The Darkness Manifesto

The Darkness Manifesto

How light pollution threatens the ancient rhythms of life

JOHAN EKLÖF

Translated from the Swedish by Elizabeth DeNoma

BH

THE BODLEY HEAD
LONDON

1 3 5 7 9 10 8 6 4 2

The Bodley Head, an imprint of Vintage, is part of the Penguin Random House group of companies whose addresses can be found at global.penguinrandomhouse.com.

Penguin Random House UK

The cost of this translation was supported by a subsidy from the Swedish Arts Council, gratefully acknowledged

Published by agreement with Sebes Bisseling Literary Agency, Amsterdam
Originally published in Sweden in 2020 by Natur & Kultur as *Mörkermanifestet*

First published by The Bodley Head in 2022

www.penguin.co.uk/vintage

A CIP catalogue record for this book is available from the British Library

Hardback ISBN 9781847927156
Trade paperback ISBN 9781847927163

Typeset in 10.5/15.5 pt Mercury Text G1 by Jouve (UK) Milton Keynes
Printed and bound in Great Britain by Clays Ltd, Elcograf S.p.A.

The authorised representative in the EEA is Penguin Random House Ireland, Morrison Chambers, 32 Nassau Street, Dublin D02 YH68

Penguin Random House is committed to a sustainable future for our business, our readers and our planet. This book is made from Forest Stewardship Council® certified paper.

FSC www.fsc.org MIX Paper from responsible sources FSC® C018179

CONTENTS

Introduction: The Disappearing Night 1

Part I: Light Pollution 5

The Cycle of Darkness 7
Experiences in Darkness 11
Illuminated Planet 15
The Vacuum Cleaner Effect 19
Extinguished Mating Impulse 23
Mass Die-off 29

Part II : The Night as an Ecological Niche 35

See in the Dark 37
The Eye 41
Nocturnal Senses 45
Twilight Animals 51
Sing in the Wrong Light 55
Nature's Own Lanterns 59
Light Spring 65
The Star Compass 71
The Dazzling City 77
False Summer 81
Fruitless Night 85

The Fireworks of the Sea 89
Where the Sea Waits 93
Romance in the Moonlight 97
Pale Coral 101
The Twilight Zone 105
Ecosystem in Flux 111
The Threat to the Bats 115
Night Services 119

Part III: Humanity and the Cosmic Light 123

Three Twilights 125
Dark Matter 131
Measure of the Night Sky 135
Saint Lawrence's Tears 139
The Only Moon? 143
The Blue Moment 147
Yellow-grey Sky 151
Industrial Light 155
When the Clocks Are Off 159
Sick with Light 165

Part IV: In Praise of Shadows 169

Like a Balm for the Soul 171
In Praise of Shadows 175
Diode Light 179
Darkness Tourism 183
The King's Darkness 189
Extinguished Conversation 193
The Darkness in the Tunnel 199
The Darkness Manifesto 203

Acknowledgements 205
Resources for Further Reading and Listening 207
Sources 209
Index 223

INTRODUCTION: THE DISAPPEARING NIGHT

My torchlight sweeps over a demon painted black with bat wings and a snake for a tail. The creature looks like it's throwing itself backwards, light radiating from its mouth, as if it has tried to swallow the light but can no longer contain its power. The creature of darkness is dying. I am in an eighteenth-century church in Sweden, painted with biblical themes, and far at the back you can find the most horrific devils and demons, put there to remind us of the torments of hell. But perhaps the church painter also wanted to tell us that we can overcome the dangers of darkness. From the church's perspective, bats are the Devil's minions, filthy animals that represent both literal and philosophical darkness, in opposition to the light of God. So it's a bit ironic that churches have so often become the nesting places of these creatures.

I continue exploring the church, climbing up a flight of stairs and stepping through a little door into the attic. On the old wooden floorboards are piles of guano and severed butterfly wings, a clear sign that the church is inhabited by the brown long-eared bat. The dusk flickering between the roof slats grows weaker, and outside the sky turns navy blue. The humid night air entering the attic carries a pleasant smell of freshly cut grass, tar and sun-warmed wood. The bats are unwilling to come out from under the eaves this early in the evening, so I go outside to meet them in the cemetery as they alight into the summer night.

One after another they take off headfirst from the roof and go straight to the nearest tree and its protective shadows. In a fitful dance, they glide, inaudible to the human ear, by the red-painted wooden church, alongside the hedges and around the treetops, searching for insects. Soon the bats will be gone, swallowed by the night.

Swedish churches and their outbuildings have largely been tended in the same way for centuries and have grown to be important havens for animals and plants in an ever-changing world. Year after year, long-eared bats have moved into turrets and attics in the early summer to give birth to new generations. In the 1980s, two-thirds of churches in Västergötland had their own bat colony. Today, forty years later, research I've done with my colleagues shows that this number has decreased by a third because of light pollution and other factors – because the churches all glow like carnivals in the night. District after district has installed modern floodlights to showcase their architectural pride. All the while, the animals – which for centuries have found safety in the darkness of the church towers and for 70 million years have made the night their abode – are slowly but surely vanishing from these places, maybe completely.

Sitting in the cemetery in the July night, I'm not only in the company of bats. I can see a hedgehog, beetles making their way up through the grass towards the starry sky and, above the headstones, caddisflies dancing like spirits. I start to relax in the shady environment, as all the impressions of the day give way to more subtle experiences and my eyes slowly acclimatise to the night. I've entered another dimension that few others ever take the time to visit.

It is not just the bats and me who enjoy the darkness. Most mammals are more active at twilight, like the hedgehog that keeps me company at this late hour. Half of the insects on this planet are nocturnal, and for the last couple of years we have been drowning in alarming reports regarding their disappearance. Forestry, environmental toxins, large-scale farming and climate change – many causes are mentioned but little is said about light, even though the light-sensitive moth belongs to one of the most affected categories. Moths looking for nectar in the darkness are easily confused by all the lights. Either they don't fly at all, believing that dawn is about to break, or they're caught in the beams of light when trying to navigate by the moon. Exhausted, they die or get killed by predators, without having fulfilled their nocturnal mission, and in that way fewer plants are pollinated. Many of us have probably seen the phenomenon out in our gardens or under a streetlight – the brighter the lights, the greater the attraction. The light lures insects from forests and villages, from the countryside and cities, depleting entire ecosystems.

Mossebo Church may lack floodlighting, but some light still reaches this place. Alongside the walking paths there are a few lights, and in the sky a faint orange glow can be seen coming from the nearest villages. This is light pollution – a collective term used for light that can be regarded as superfluous but still has a great impact on our lives and our ecosystems.

The term was coined by astronomers but is today used by ecologists, physiologists and neurologists who study the effects of the disappearing night. It is no longer just a question of stars and insects. It is about all living things, including we humans. Ever since the birth of our planet, day has been followed by night, and every cell in every living organism has built-in machinery working in harmony with that rhythm. The natural light calibrates our inner circadian rhythm and controls hormones and bodily processes.

Up until about 150 years ago, when the light bulb was invented, these processes were allowed to develop slowly and without disturbance. But today there are ominous signs of how streetlights and floodlights supersede natural night light and disturb this ancient circadian rhythm. The artificial light, the polluting light, is now dominant – the light that causes birds to sing in the middle of the night, sends baby turtles in the wrong direction and prevents corals' mating rituals, which take place under the light of the moon.

Humanity's desire to illuminate the world makes the earth, viewed from space, glow in the night. Every city and every street is visible a long way out into the cosmic darkness, which is perhaps one of the most obvious signs that we have entered a new era: the Anthropocene, the time of humans. Beneath the illuminated sky in the illuminated cities we have created, we can no longer see any stars, and many of us don't remember what the Milky Way looks like. We are missing out on one of nature's grandest treasures – the spectacles of the sky with its breathtaking perspectives, its falling stars and, on occasion, its strikingly beautiful northern lights.

Light pollution is still a term unknown to many, but at the same time, it's an exploding field of research, and light will probably soon be as strictly regulated as noise. The LED, the modern diode, which has enabled the explosion of lighting in private gardens and industrial car parks, could also be a solution to the problem. Light and dark is not a matter of black or white. We can programme and dim artificial light and adapt it to more natural conditions – if we want to.

With this book, I examine the impact that darkness and the night have on all living creatures. In concise chapters, I'll share my experiences and thoughts stemming from my twenty years in the service of the night, as a bat researcher, traveller and friend of the darkness. I hope that this book will inspire others, function as a reminder of the importance of letting the night be a part of our lives and give insight into how much damage artificial light can do – a stirring manifesto for natural darkness.

PART I:
LIGHT POLLUTION

THE CYCLE OF DARKNESS

Mimosa pudica has an odd quality. The plant is sensitive to being touched, and if you brush against its leaves, it closes like an umbrella and seems to wither before your eyes. The same thing happens at night. Every morning it opens up and turns its leaves like satellite dishes to capture the sunlight, and at night it once again resumes its sleeping position. The French scientist Jean-Jacque d'Ortous de Mairan (1678–1771) placed a specimen in constant darkness, only to discover that the leaves still opened when it was daylight outside, even though the plant saw nothing of the sun. He interpreted this to mean that the plant was in some way still able to feel the sun's presence. How this could be, de Mairan never quite managed to explain.

It was only during the second half of the last century, with the breakthrough of genetics, that the mystery was solved. In the 1960s, the biologist and geneticist Michael W. Young had begun to ponder the mimosa plants' and other plants' behaviour during different times of the day, and from this pondering a lifelong interest in the biological clock was born. In 2017, Young, along with Jeffrey C. Hall and Michael Rosbash, won the Nobel Prize in Physiology or Medicine. They had succeeded in isolating the gene that controls a rhythm in all living things, from bacteria to human beings. The *circadian* rhythm, which can be thought of as our internal food and sleep clock, has been with us since the beginning of time, following the day's natural oscillation between darkness to light and back again.

Over billions of years – the earth is four and a half billion years old – our planet has changed form, slowly or in sudden events. Mountain ranges and seas are formed, rivers are moved, and species are born and die out. Not even the magnetic poles constitute fixed points. Right now, the magnetic North Pole is moving eastwards, from northern Canada towards Siberia, at a speed of 11 kilometres per year. But one thing has remained more or less constant: the alternation between day and night, between light and darkness. The sun has always gone down in the west and risen again in the east, and in between those moments it has always been night.

The length of a day in itself has not always been the same. Modern atomic clocks tell us that the speed of the earth's rotation is slowly decreasing, and the days are actually becoming longer. A slightly longer period of day, a slightly longer night. The rate of change is not especially dramatic and amounts to barely two milliseconds per century. But if the day has always changed at the same rate, the earth's very first life forms, living more than three billion years ago, experienced a day that was only half as long as ours.

There are many theories about where this first life arose, a life that was not much more than self-copying molecules: in the deep sea, under thick ice, far inside mountain crevices in a mass of mud, or potentially even in some other place in the universe entirely. But wherever life first came about, the first single-celled organisms developed quickly and found new possibilities in the unexplored world.

Soon *cyanobacteria*, bacteria with the ability to use sunlight to create oxygen, spread over the world's oceans. Every morning, when the sun's first rays warmed the surface of the water, cyanobacteria, which we also know as blue-green algae, gathered the light's energy and released oxygen into the atmosphere. They played a crucial role in the atmosphere's chemical composition, allowing animal life, including humans, to develop. Cyanobacteria's inner machinery laid the foundations for plant development and photosynthesis, and their rhythm has propagated itself through generation after generation.

The earth's first multicellular life saw the light of day 620 million years ago, when a day cycle was around twenty-two hours long. Although, they didn't literally see the light of day. It would still be millions of years before eyes or any other truly advanced senses existed. During this time, totally unique organisms that died out more than half a billion years ago thrived. But for millions of years, they could live a quiet life on luxuriant carpets of algae, without risk of predators and without needing to move a millimetre. Every day, sunshine trickled through the surface water and changed character on its way to the deep. Every evening, the effects of the light stopped, and the natural night took hold. Life adapted to these shifts.

The biological clock, the circadian rhythm, is ancient, shared and completely fundamental. Everything living today has developed in a world where the conditions change over the day and over the year. Our bodies simply expect light and dark in recurrently longer and shorter cycles. Every organism makes use of the pre-programmed clock in different ways: when the mimosa plant collapses its leaves, the butterfly orchid wakes up to life and boosts its scent in order to attract moths. The bee and other daytime insects end their shift, and the night pollinators begin. All employ the same foundational mechanism, regardless of species, habitat or life cycle, from 2.5-billion-year-old cyanobacteria to bats to humans.

Light and darkness calibrate the biological clock. Without information about changes in the surroundings, the inner mechanism continues to pulse in regular rhythm for about a day. The morning light signals that the cycle must begin again from zero, that a new day has just begun. The clock continues over the day, through dusk towards night, the whole time with input from the sun's changing light. The artificial light from streetlamps, headlights and floodlights is, of course, not in this equation and risks, to put it mildly, creating disorder in the system.

EXPERIENCES IN DARKNESS

I usually begin my nightly itinerary by sitting down in a peaceful place, preferably near some water. I pour a cup of coffee from my flask and let my mind passively take in the impressions of twilight. The steam from the coffee mingles with the fog over the water as darkness falls and still air cools near the surface. The birdsong grows more sparse, the long-horned grasshopper's hoarse sound becomes sharper, and the forest builds a dark green backdrop. During summer in Scandinavia, the day's transformation to night can carry on a long while, as a subtle displacement of light and activity, where the day's animals meet the night's, where the songbirds' warble hardly falls off before the woodcock arrives in swift flight. In the tropics, the shift occurs rapidly, like when the staging in a theatre is changed. The spotlight is replaced with shadow, and the stage and audience are the same, but the actors are new.

Sometimes it takes a while for the bats to show up. Here, patience is paramount. I want to believe that I work more effectively in the long run if I let natural pauses happen, if I let the darkness fall in its own time. The natural experience does not necessarily make me a better fieldworker, but it makes me one who is more tuned in. If I allowed internet surfing and my mobile phone to disturb me with their light and audible pings, I would lose both focus and my night vision.

The fact is that I, unwilling to lose my night vision, seldom even use a head torch, at least not outside. Otherwise, I'd not have seen the ground beetles hunting small insects or the spiderwebs glittering in their special way in the moonlight. A lot would have passed me by, like the slugs moving themselves along and the mushrooms lighting up. Indeed, some fungi have *bioluminescence*, the quality that gets sea-fire and glow worms to gleam in the dark. With this light they attract flies, beetles and ants that spread their spores. The phenomenon is most common in the tropics, but here in Sweden there is the illuminating honey fungus, whose mycelium, which is a fungus's threadlike growth network, glows a dim green. It's been said that people in earlier eras could use wood from oaks overtaken by fungal mycelia to show them the way at night. Maybe other mushrooms stand out like lanterns for animals with better night vision than ours.

It is fascinating to imagine how nocturnal animals experience their existence in the dark, how their brains interpret sensory stimuli. In my vicinity, hundreds of normally invisible white flowers called Nottingham catchflies glitter when the moon shows itself. It is beautiful in a subtle way, but to animals with sensitivity to the ultraviolet spectrum the ground shines like a fluorescent dance-floor. As humans – with our senses' specific limitations – we can never, though we know about these animals' visual faculty, envisage the real experience of it. Filters in cameras or visual enhancement through other machines give us an inkling, but we can never completely see with the eyes of insects or cats. The philosopher Thomas Nagel wrote in the 1970s in his famous essay 'What is it like to be a bat?' that human language can describe what it's like to be a bat as little as it can describe what it's like to be an extraterrestrial. Only individuals from the same species can understand each other's experiences, and if we extend Nagel's reasoning, we really cannot know what it is like to be another human being either. We only have our own senses, filters and interpretations.

But if you remove yourself from the fast lane, sit down as an observer and let the darkness meet you, proximity to nocturnal life nevertheless becomes more striking. Senses other than sight take hold, and slowly the sounds and smells change, the air becomes damp against your skin. A nightjar, a bird of twilight, flies past with a suggestive, unmistakable drone. Some frogs croak, a far-off black-throated loon calls out its melancholy verse, and at a distance, a splash in still water can be heard. Gradually, your night vision also improves, and you get an idea of how flowers of the dark come to life, such as the white campion, butterfly orchid and night-flowering catchfly. They release their scent molecules and spores into the wind for nocturnal pollinators to follow. It is during early summer's drawn-out twilight that the lilac comes most fully into its own, and it's said that a person born around midnight can see ghosts in the lilac's silhouette on Sundays. In August, the smell of wild capriole takes over the summer night, and owlet moths are drawn towards its characteristic blossoms along the scent trail. With their long, sucking proboscis, the moths slake their thirst on nectar and pollinate the plant. Moths have the animal world's most exceptional sense of smell and can capture separate scent molecules with their antennae, in this way finding a flower or a partner from several kilometres away. Allow yourself to sit outside during twilight, and you'll soon get a feeling for the invisible scent trails by observing the moths' strenuous flight. Moths have shown themselves to be at least as important pollinators as the diurnal bees, and they even visit more kinds of flowers than bees do, something of utmost importance for keeping our ecosystem intact and thriving.

One of the moths I'm observing suddenly takes a sharp dive towards the ground and then pulls an acrobatic loop to return to its scent trail again. Moths have developed hearing that enables them to hear the sounds from the very bats I am here to inventory. So their sudden jerks are flights from the enemy. In my ultrasound detector, which makes the bats' sounds audible for human beings, their search pulses rattle like exploding popcorn. The closer the moth, the faster the bats cry out to locate the prey. Moths veer and feint in a duel under the night sky, accompanied by a measured rhythm. On the ground, several beetles rush forwards. There's rustling in the leaves and soon two cockchafers rise in a mating dance. For a moment, the buzz of their beating wings overpowers the sounds from the ultrasound detector.

No less than a third of all vertebrates and almost two-thirds of all invertebrates are nocturnal, so it's after we humans fall asleep that most natural activity occurs in the form of mating, hunting, decomposing and pollinating. As a bat researcher, I'm regularly reminded of how little we still know about the night and its secrets, about the bats co-ordinating flight around trees, about how they determine in a microsecond what the landscape around them looks like using only sound and its echo. The darkness is not the world of humans. We're only visitors.

ILLUMINATED PLANET

The bat, the nightjar and the cockchafer all belong to twilight, while the human being, to the utmost degree, is a diurnal animal. We are in many ways completely dependent on visual sensory impressions, and light therefore means safety to us. So it isn't strange that we tend to want to light up our existence, and with the triumphant march of electricity and the light bulb across the world in the last 150 years, and now with revolutionary diode lamps, this illumination is occurring at an ever-higher rate. We light gardens, streets, industrial areas and car parks with street-lamps, floodlights and string lights, often with safety in mind. In the school car park a few hundred metres from where I live, they've put up about fifty lampposts. That's more than one lamp-post per 10 square metres of asphalt, mostly for the enjoyment of motoring young people, who drive there to have a place to socialise at night. And it looks the same everywhere; light shines from empty offices, in vacant car parks and on the facades of warehouses along our motorways. Human beings have extended their day, and at the same time they have forced out the night's inhabitants.

Nightly satellite pictures of the earth show a planet that glows. All the world's densely populated areas form brightly lit spots that can be seen far out into space. Lighted roadways bind cities together in a shining network, and the most densely lit parts make a single haze. Satellite pictures show in a very concrete way how the urbanised world spreads itself out and are perhaps the strongest symbols of the Anthropocene in which we find ourselves. The concept was developed in the 1980s and later popularised by the Dutch chemist and Nobel Prize-winner Paul Crutzen to designate the epoch in which we are living. To name a new geological epoch after human influence over the world isn't a new idea. It can be traced back to the 1860s and George Perkins Marsh (1801–82), an American politician, diplomat and linguist who, somewhat unexpectedly, came to be a foundational figure in an early environmental movement. Influenced by his 1864 book *Man and Nature: or, Physical Geography as Modified by Human Action*, the next two decades saw a succession of attempts to pick up on the concept of humans' virulent effects on the environment and name the ruling epoch after them. But it's only now that the ideas of the Anthropocene have really taken hold.

Nightly satellite pictures give a clear view of how modern human activity is spreading in time and space. Even though there is, of course, much good to say about what technological developments have done for human beings – with their actual as well as symbolic illuminations – it is also plain to see that in their tracks follow energy wastage, rampant consumerism and ecological degradation. What we call light pollution, that is to say superfluous artificial light, changes nature's inherited conditions and has hitherto been an underappreciated feature of the Anthropocene. But artificial lighting today makes up a tenth of our total energy usage, and only an extremely small part of the light is of actual benefit to us, as most of it spills out into the sky instead of lighting walkways and outer doors as intended. Research shows that badly directed and unnecessarily strong lights in Europe and the US are equivalent to the carbon dioxide emissions of nearly 20 million cars. In 2017, it was estimated that light pollution increases by a minimum of 2 per cent globally each year.

One of the reasons for our eagerness to illuminate our planet so persistently is without a doubt our nyctophobia – fear of the dark. To be afraid of the dark lies in our genetic, as well as our cultural, heritage. It is altogether natural and, just like many other fears, has a survival value. We certainly can adapt our sense of sight so that we see decently in the dark, but it's a slow process. It takes at least half an hour for the right pigment to build up in our eyes when the daylight's bombardment of photons has begun to decrease, and a little while more before we reach our maximum light sensitivity and we can orient ourselves in the dark. And the heightened sensitivity to darkness can be undone in an instant. One look at a streetlight, a mobile phone turning on or a passing car's headlights breaks down the rhodopsin, our light-sensitive visual pigment; the sensitivity falls like a house of cards and the eye is forced to begin again.

In our cities today, it is almost impossible to establish true night vision, for there are far too many points of light, which effectively hinder the build-up of rhodopsin. In Hong Kong and Singapore, which are considered the earth's brightest cities, or maybe more specifically the most light-polluted, there's barely a street corner where it's dark enough to call forth the eye's natural night vision. People in Hong Kong sleep under a night sky that is 1,200 times brighter than the unilluminated sky, and if you were raised in Singapore, you've likely never experienced what it's like to have developed night vision. This is applying to more and more of us who live in cities, wherever in the world we find ourselves.

The loss of the experience of night can possibly seem nostalgic and tangential. But there's a lot of research showing that the human being in the Anthropocene experiences highly negative effects from too much artificial light. The light disturbs our biological clock, leading to sleeping difficulties, depression and obesity. There have also been studies that show that certain forms of cancer can be a direct effect of too much light at night. But we'll further explore all of this later.

THE VACUUM CLEANER EFFECT

A moth steers towards a shimmering waterfall and disappears into the water. Soon another one comes along, and before long a whole trail of moths appears. None of them hesitates or stops, and they continue straight into the rushing water.

The observation was made at the Icelandic waterfall Skjálfandafljót in the 1800s. It wasn't the need to cool off that enticed the moths that night, nor was it their inevitable death. It was the shine and glitter from the fall's water droplets, the hypnotic power of attraction, that drew the moths in. George John Romanes (1848–94), philosopher, psychologist and biologist, studied instincts in both humans and animals and was fascinated by how the weakest light – from a glowing matchstick or a glittering droplet of water – could draw insects off course. Romanes was working at Oxford University and was a close friend of Charles Darwin. He was also an eager spokesman for Darwin's theories and was predicted to be his successor on evolution's throne.

Unfortunately, George John Romanes died at the early age of forty-six, gradually landing in the shadow of other biologists working in the field in the next century. But his ideas about animal instinct in his works *Mental Evolution in Animals* and *Mental Evolution in Man* have had a large influence within both zoology and psychology. And in the same way that Romanes made note of how moths were drawn to the shimmering body of water at Skjálfandafljót, most of us have at some point observed insects that were drawn to a light source come closer to it, little by little in ever tighter circles, finally to fall straight down into the centre.

In 2001, I took part in a workshop about bats in Krau Wildlife Reserve in Malaysia's interior forest. As a young graduate student halfway through my dissertation, I didn't want to miss the experience. There was a local television crew on location, which followed one of the domestic researchers in his work with bats. One evening, during dinner, one of the crewmembers' large lights was left on, directed up towards the sky. This created a compact column of light in the dark, humid rainforest air and showed with tremendous clarity what happens to insect fauna around a light source. A heavy stream of moths, caddisflies, mosquitoes, beetles, crickets and all manner of more or less obscure insects were caught in the light, and one by one they danced in a spiral down towards the source. Although not all of them, actually. One opportunistic praying mantis had landed on the edge, now raking in endless prey. The praying mantis had transformed the light into its own private trap, and I sat for a long time studying its seemingly conscious efforts.

At the south end of the Las Vegas Strip, the city's most famous street, a towering light installation functions in much the same way. Atop the Luxor Hotel and Casino sits what is America's, and likely the world's, most powerful illuminated object – the Luxor Sky Beam. With the help of a complex of curved mirrors and thirty-nine xenon lights at 7,000 watts each, a beam points right into space and can be seen nearly 40 kilometres away, at least if you are at the cruising altitude of an aeroplane. The strength of the light is equivalent to 42 billion candles. If you're going to stand out in one of the world's brightest cities, it doesn't do to skimp on power.

After an unusually damp 2019 – at least by Nevada's standards – an enormous grasshopper migration was triggered in the area. Grasshopper swarms of this kind are in themselves nothing unusual, and the same thing happened in East Africa half a year later. Many species of grasshoppers happily migrate in large numbers, especially after seasons with a lot of rain. The grasshoppers can multiply quickly and create enormous populations in a short time, and when they reach a certain population size, their hormone system tells them it is time to move. The massive number of grasshoppers not only forms a spectacle but can also present great societal problems, not least by destroying crops. It's difficult not to draw connections to the Bible in this case! A hotel in the form of an Egyptian pyramid, a sin city characterised by gaming and gambling, and a swarm of millions of grasshoppers that sweeps in from the surrounding deserts, as in one of God's ten plagues from the Book of Exodus. Social media was, not unpredictably, full of fantastic film clips and commentary in July 2019, when the invasion reached its climax.

The grasshoppers normally migrate at night, and every evening Nevada's meteorologists could see the swarms approach Las Vegas on their radar screens. All the city's lights, advertising screens and neon signs were like magnets for the grasshoppers, and worst of all, of course, was the Luxor Sky Beam, which attracted individual insects all the way from Arizona. In insect circles, people usually talk about the *vacuum cleaner effect*. And precisely like the Luxor Sky Beam and the light I studied in the Malaysian forest, every streetlight, every porch light and every illuminated facade functioned as a magnet for insects. On a larger scale, cities attract insects from rural areas, which leads to changes throughout the entire ecosystem.

The vacuum cleaner effect has long been used by entomologists to capture insects with light traps. These consist in principle of a light and a box, and when the insects come flying, they are captured in a funnel and sealed in. This kind of trap sat on the roof of the Swedish Museum of Natural History between 1990 and 2007. Every year, the lamp was visited by over two hundred kinds of butterflies and altogether over the seventeen years no fewer than 740 different species. Apart from butterfly species, beetles and heteropteran were also counted. Over the course of years, the composition of species did not change to any great extent; approximately the same sorts of nocturnal insects got caught in the trap on the roof. But if those researchers had noted the number of individuals of each species and weighed them, that is to say measured the amount of biomass, they probably could have perceived a trend. In Germany, the same type of measurement was introduced a year earlier in a study of a considerably larger scope. In more than sixty different nature reserves, insects were captured, identified by species and weighed. And in 2013, the first warning came.

But it wasn't until four years later, after further data analysis, that the news reached the rest of the world. It then spread quickly via social media with subject lines such as 'Armageddon' and 'Insect collapse'; the biomass of insects had decreased by 75 per cent! The results were published in Open Access, available for everyone who wanted to draw their own conclusions, reinterpret the statistics or review competing research. But the conclusion is clear: the number of insects is decreasing. The reasons for insect death are many, from urbanisation and global warming to insecticides, large-scale farming, monoculture and disappearing forests. Probably all these factors play a role. But to everyone who's ever seen an insect react to light, it is obvious that light pollution is a major cause.

EXTINGUISHED MATING IMPULSE

No one knows exactly how many insect species there are in the world; it's a question of millions, and new ones are constantly being discovered. In Sweden and Norway alone, 1,600 completely new species of insect have been identified in the last decade. In the tropics, every insect inventory leads to new discoveries and many species presumably die out before we even have time to meet them.

Half of all species of insect are nocturnal and need at least several continuous hours of darkness to be able to obtain food and find a mate. The night's limited light is these insects' protection, and the pale glow from the stars and moon are central for their navigation and hormonal system. Disturbances in the natural oscillation between light and dark is therefore a threat to the night insects' very existence.

In order to navigate the night, the majority of insects use the stars, the moon or so-called polarised light. A moth during flight in the darkness keeps a straight course by maintaining contact with the moon, the brightest source of natural light in the night sky. The moth simply maintains a constant bearing with the moon in order to know where it is heading. When it instead comes upon a light, an unnatural element in the moth's existence that is infinitely closer than the moon, the moth is going to slowly turn towards the light in order to continue at the same bearing. It results in flight spiralling closer and closer to the light.

When insects have been caught in the hypnotising light, they stay there. Many of them die before dawn, sometimes of sheer exhaustion. When the lights eventually turn off, often at the same time as the sun returns, the surviving insects have hardly moved at all and haven't achieved their night's goals. They haven't got their nectar, haven't transported the plants' pollen around, haven't found a partner or haven't been able to lay any eggs.

Another effective way to find the way through the night's darkness is with the help of polarised light. This is frequently employed by insects, but maybe even humans have made use of the same trick in the past. In the Icelandic sagas, for example, it's been shown how the Vikings could navigate over the seas using a crystal called a sunstone. The stone revealed an unseen pattern in the sky, formed by the light from the sun's rays. No matter the weather, the Vikings could see where the sun was as long as they looked through the crystal. Archaeologists have never found such a sunstone, but in theory it should work.

Light waves undulate in all planes, not just up and down or side to side. Each plane is followed equally as long as the light travels unhindered. But when the photons meet the molecules and particles in the air, or when the light passes, for example, a water surface, some of the planes are filtered out, the light becomes polarised and the light waves swing, or vibrate, more in one plane than in others. This, of course, is happening all the time, and across the sky a pattern of light is formed that swings in different planes and has been polarised to different degrees. As the sun goes down, the polarisation changes accordingly, and at dawn and dusk the pattern is least complex. It's as if the sun pulls its rays with it over the edge of the earth and leaves trails on the evening sky, trails that are both a compass and a clock. We human beings don't see them with our naked eye, but insects do, and furthermore, they can use them to orient themselves.

We've long known that bees benefit from polarised light, but more recently we have discovered that a long line of insects, spiders, crustaceans and even birds make use of the optical compass. Also, when the sun has long since sunk below the horizon, the moon can give the same effect, although its glow is 400,000 times weaker than the sun's.

The dung beetle is one of the best at using the moon's barely discernible light pattern in the sky. There are many different dung beetles, with some sixty species in Sweden alone. Most known are probably the dung beetles that make balls of animal droppings, which they then effectively roll away with them over the African savannah. Using its back legs, the beetle assiduously pushes the ball to its nest. The ball can weigh many times its own weight, and a ball full of nourishment is a desirable booty for other dung beetles, which is reason to rush home. In order to find the shortest and fastest way, the dung beetles navigate with help from the moon's polarised light in the night sky, and even the weakest light from the sliver of a new moon can lead them in the right direction. They have such great sensitivity for nuanced differences in this light that even in environments close to big cities where traces of light spill out from streets and houses, they can find their way. But then it's a requirement for the moon to be full, for otherwise the trails in the sky are hidden, even for dung beetles. For safety's sake, they also make use of the stars, however, to orient themselves in the open landscape. By climbing up on their ball, turning towards space and performing a little dance they create for themselves a snapshot of the sky, like an astrophoto of the night's heavenly pattern. Giant crab spiders in desert areas do something similar. By calmly watching the night sky with their eight eyes, they create a picture of the horizon and the positions of the stars, a star map, which helps them find their way among the desolate sand dunes.

When the dung beetle has sculpted its ball of manure, memorised the night's star images and determined its direction, it rolls its ball home to safety in a straight line. In ancient Egypt, people believed that the dung beetles, the *scarabs*, laid their eggs in the ball, and therefore in that culture they became holy symbols of fertility. The dung beetles' journey was likened to the sun's path across the heavens, which is why the sun god Ra's morning form, Khepri, is usually drawn with a dung beetle head.

When light strikes a water surface, the light waves are reflected in a distinct polarised pattern, by which caddisflies, diving beetles and other water insects can navigate to find bodies of water. But artificial light can create false water surfaces. Asphalt, concrete, glass and the glossy coatings on cars all reflect light in a waterlike way, and the artificial lights from houses, shopping centres and industrial areas strengthen the effect. I have found diving beetles on the hood of my car and seen mayflies land in car parks to lay eggs. The mayflies' short adult life largely has no other purpose than to give the new generation good conditions in which to thrive by laying eggs on water. Distracting the insects with industrial areas or large car parks can be an effective way to knock out entire populations overnight.

Aside from disturbing the insects' natural navigation and, in the worst cases, luring them to complete inactivity or death, artificial light can even impede their production of *pheromones*, scent secretions that they send out to locate and communicate with other members of their species. The darkness at twilight is the signal for the hormonal system to activate. The lights turn mating impulses off, and the night's scent trails fail to appear.

One species afflicted by this is the cabbage moth, a big,

speckled moth that is found throughout much of Europe and Asia. The adult cabbage moth crawls out of its chrysalis in May and June, and not many minutes pass before it begins to search for a partner. The female takes the first step by extending her antennae forwards, flapping her wings and emitting scent secretions. The time will be around ten o'clock in the evening. A male interprets the scent and does the same, pulls back his antennae, makes several rapid wing movements and sets out to find the good-smelling female. When they meet, the male brushes against the female's body with his antennae in order to feel if he has found the right mate. Then he resumes his rapid wing-flapping, and the mating is initiated. They spend the night together, the female's wing around the male's body, after which she leaves to lay the fertilised eggs.

The entire mating ritual occurs in the dark. In the laboratory environment, it has been observed that the female emits fewer pheromones in the presence of artificial light and, furthermore, that the composition of the scent secretion looks completely different compared to when surrounded by darkness. So the mating never gets started. The females wait in vain in the darkness, the males wait in vain for the right scent. The larvae that do manage to be produced and that eventually pupate risk hatching prematurely. Darkness is also crucial for them. Long nights are important for maintaining rest in the pupa stage, and the light the larvae are exposed to causes them to transform into moths too soon. They can also hatch in autumn or winter, when there's no food available. Light, or the absence of darkness, simply betrays the insects in all their life stages and leads them to death.

MASS DIE-OFF

Aside from the previously mentioned German study, there are other indicators that there are alarming developments in the world's insect population. Anyone who, like me, is old enough to have driven a car during the previous century has experienced the problem of dead insects on the front bumper and headlights. Earlier studies indicate that as many as hundreds of billions of insects may have died each year on speeding cars with illuminated headlights in the dark of night. Anyone still driving a car can, however, attest to the fact that the problem has decreased: not as many insects get stuck on the car. That's called the windscreen phenomenon, and it's a tangible, if anecdotal, observation about the number of insects in the vicinity of our roads. We see it in Sweden, in England, throughout Europe, in the US, in the tropics – everywhere. Often it's amateur entomologists, butterfly collectors and field biologists on excursions who've accumulated this type of data, and there are as yet few long-term studies on the subject. But a Danish researcher, Anders Pape Møller, put his own car and its windscreen to use in measuring the change in the amount of insects. Over a period of twenty years, he drove the same distance and found a significant decrease in the quantity of insects, which also corresponds to the decrease in the number of insect-eating birds during the same period of time. Møller was thus able to show that the windscreen phenomenon was real, and with it grew the incentives to take the problem seriously.

Otherwise, there's more meaningful research into how to kill insects than into how to save them, which is fairly telling about how we humans operate. For example, there are well-documented tests of how you overcome pests with light traps.

Measuring the biomass of insects in Germany wasn't initiated by the state of the university, either. It was the members of the *Entomologischer Verein Krefeld*, the Krefeld Insect Society, who began this substantial work. The association was formed as early as 1905 and as such has performed its duty in the interests of insects for over a century. Fifty members with a collection of nearly one million insects between them crowded into their meeting room in an old school building in central Krefeld, North Rhine-Westphalia. Ten times more insects can now be found in labelled jars, stacked in the classrooms like chaotic museum exhibits, and the collections have cultural-historical protection. The members are not educated zoologists. They are instead priests, publishers, technicians and teachers, all of whom, however, are prominent in their respective areas. One of the association's more renowned members, Siegfried Cymorek (1927–87), for example, was awarded an honorary doctorate in Zurich, though he never graduated from primary school. The association has published over two thousand articles on insects, taxonomy and ecology, and today, as a result of their sounding the alarm about insect die-off in 2013, the research world has woken up and supports the association in its project. The interest in insect studies has also exploded at universities worldwide.

Life on earth has collapsed five times. The last time it happened was 65 million years ago when the dinosaurs disappeared along with three-quarters of the rest of the animal population. Today, about 40 per cent of all insect species are threatened with extinction and an Australian-Chinese compilation of the collected world insect data from 2019 shows that we're moving towards the earth's sixth mass extinction. And humanity is the cause. Of all the different insect groups studied, it turned out to have been the worst for different varieties of moth. Among these, more than two-thirds of species are on a negative trend and a third are acutely endangered. The authors of the article write in an interview that the number of insect species decreases by almost 3 per cent annually, which, if the pace continues, would imply that in a hundred years there'll be barely any at all, with great peril for the earth's ecosystem.

A few years ago, photographs of orchards in Chinese Sichuan showed thousands of workers equipped with brushes as they climbed trees to hand-pollinate blossoms – work that should have been performed by bees. A fast worker was expected to pollinate about ten trees a day, whereas a small colony of bees can handle a hundred times more. We don't know if the employment office will be looking for pollinators for our crops in the future, but with fewer and fewer insects in the wild, it is inevitable that mankind will be impacted.

The insect die-off discovered by the members of the Krefeld Insect Society was initially not associated with light pollution, despite its close proximity to the industrial cities of the Ruhr area and to Europe's most densely populated country, the Netherlands. This is partly due to the fact that many of the affected insect groups are diurnal. But while the German analyses were in full swing and the decrease in flower pollination was evident, some Dutch researchers observed in the journal *Global Change Biology* that moths, which of course fly in the dark, seem to have decreased more than other insect groups. And the decrease was particularly striking in urban environments. It started to be clear that light was an important piece of the puzzle.

Ecologists from the United States and Canada soon began collaborating with their colleagues from Australia and New Zealand. They were all convinced that light played a greater role than had been demonstrated before. After all, the circadian cycle is the factor that would normally have been the most constant thing in the whole ecosystem. That is until we started using artificial light. Working together, the research team ensured that they gathered all the available research about insects and light in an attempt to get an overview of the situation. Their compilation showed that there were already about a hundred scientific articles published in which there were claims that artificial light adversely affects insects in one way or another.

Artificial light can prolong or shorten reproductive cycles, induce hatching and affect metamorphosis – the insect's transformation from larva to pupa to mature individual. It can also change the conditions for hunting and pollination and affect food intake, flight and migration – in short, all the stages of an insect's life.

If we turn back the clock to the beginning of the twenty-first century, the phrase *light pollution* was virtually unknown. To anyone other than astronomers, that is. There were occasional studies on how light affected birds and turtles, but not much more than that. Not even bat researchers used to talk about the impact of light on their subjects. Yet we're still just at the beginning. We still know too little about how light and dark affect our ecosystems. Too few real experiments and studies have been done on too few groups of organisms. A good subject are spiders, which are often active in the evening and at night. A spider can easily be awakened or put into an inactive state through the use of light. They are never restless during the day or sleepy at night. In the spider world, it's just off or on. So they comprise a perfect study group for light pollution and are high on the list of animals that the world's relatively few circadian (light-dark) biologists would like to study.

There's a whole world out there governed by small changes in natural light, ecosystems that are woken up and set off by different times and programmed by different light intensities and wavelengths. One animal falls asleep, another animal's work begins, and chains of events, hormone cycles and behaviours begin and end when the light shows exactly what time of day it is, in what to us are sometimes very subtle ways.

With increased knowledge also come improved conditions for solutions. The more attention on the impact of light on ecological systems and our own well-being, the closer we'll get to reconciling society's need for light with nature's need for darkness.

PART II : THE NIGHT AS AN ECOLOGICAL NICHE

SEE IN THE DARK

The first eyes saw the world 540 million years ago. The ancient times came to an end and were replaced by the eon known as the Phanerozoic, which, loosely translated from Greek, means 'visible life'. And that's exactly what this eon is all about.

Everything happened during a period of ten million years. Suddenly the animals were simply there, and there were lots of them, too. It's called the *Cambrian explosion*. For a long time, it was thought that this period was the very origin of multicellular animals, because fossils found in mountains all over the earth show such a clear boundary between Precambrian and Cambrian, going from almost no animals at all to a huge abundance of animals over a geologic night. However, multicellular animals had existed long before that. There have been many theories about the background to the Cambrian explosion, but what's considered today by many people to be perhaps the most important explanation is the arrival of predation, that is animals beginning to eat each other. The genetics were there, the individual life forms were there, but the physical variations between them were few. All individuals resembled each other and did the same things in similar ways, until the threat of being eaten started to loom over them. The Cambrian is like the big bang for visible life. The building blocks for the multiplicity of life had been around for a long time, but animals began to take form in earnest after the explosion.

It was now that the animals began to be able to actually move. They also developed protective spikes and hard shells, shells that have been fossilised for us to contemplate half a billion years later. But perhaps even more importantly, the evolution of sensory organs took off, as did the arms race between predators and prey. To hear, smell and feel vibrations and see where other individuals are gives a natural head start in the struggle for survival and fertilisation. The contest between prey and predators has been evolution's strongest driving force ever since.

It was also now that the first real eyes took shape. The ability to see conveyed a huge advantage over competitors – to detect prey, to notice animals on the hunt. Although the ability to respond to light already existed, it was only now that rudimentary image vision suddenly developed. Previously, the various life forms had more or less hovered in the dark, hidden from each other. But in the Cambrian, animals could capture photons from sunlight, filtered through lenses and becoming light on their retinas. We find traces of this development in rock deposits from China, North America and also Sweden.

I camped for a summer on the slopes of the Kakeled quarry on Kinnekulle Mountain, among the mounds of petroleum-scented stone slabs in black clay slate that stuck up like charred history books. I was looking for fossils below the vertical walls of the quarry, which effectively concealed the light from nearby villages and farms. Only the summer night's reflection on Lake Vänern provided the light needed for my evening tasks. Here, where sandstone turns into alum shale, the geological story of Sweden's journey from the southern tropics to its current northern position was evident. The journey has taken half a billion years, and there are many animals that have been fossilised in the mountains along the way. The black alum slate contains snapshots of life in the Cambrian. The fossils look like hieroglyphs in the blackness, sometimes rust-red from oxidation in the slabs of iridescent green slate.

The slag heaps of stone slabs around the Kakeled quarry and other alum shale quarries on Kinnekulle are called *rödfyr* and are remnants from a bygone era during which alum shale was burned in large kilns. The high organic content of undecayed animals makes the stone an efficient fuel, and these kinds of lime kilns still stand in many quarries. In addition to energy, they also extracted alum from the shale; alum is a salt that has been used medicinally, as an anticoagulant among other things, but more than anything else, it's a dye for textiles.

Two hundred years earlier, roughly 50 kilometres from my slate mounds in Kakeled, there worked a former blacksmith's son called Sven Malmberg, and a woman called Stina Andersdotter. They were employed as a servant and a maid at the region's oldest alum quarry. The quarry is located in Dimbo parish, whose main town, also called Dimbo, is referenced as early as the 1100s. The place name comes from the Old Swedish word *dimber*, which means 'mist', 'hard to see', 'fog'. The brook, which used to be called Dimma, might have contributed to the haze over the areas around the mill. The fog, the smoke from the quarry, and the petroleum-smelling slate must have given the area a surreal look, perhaps as if Gjöll himself, the underworld river in Norse mythology, ran through here.

The work was hard and dangerous. There were quantities of uranium and arsenic seeping out of the slate that contaminated the water in the vicinity. But Sven Malmberg and Stina Andersdotter found each other in that environment and quickly became a couple. Within a short time, they'd have a son, Johannes Svensson, and then a grandson, Johan, who was my grandfather's father and my namesake. I'll have cause to return to him later in the book.

Contained in the black slate are pieces of lime that smell of petroleum, called *orsten* or 'stink stone' due to their unmistakable fragrance. The *orsten* consist entirely of shell remains and 500-million-year-old creatures, not large but so well preserved that the Västergötland orsten site has become a *Lagerstätte*, an esteemed classification designating exceptional richness and value to palaeontology. If you break open an *orsten*, a 500-million-year-old cemetery is exposed and a huge number of fossilised animals appears.

Among other things, you can see different species of the now-extinct trilobites, but also various crustaceans of fairly similar shape to those we see in our oceans today. There are alternately adults, fully developed individuals and larval forms in different stages. And there are not just shells but bones, antennae and parts of mouths and eyes. Under a microscope, the very first advanced visual organs on earth are revealed, and not just from one group of animals but from a number of different kinds of animals with varying family histories. In the *orsten*, you can chart the development of the eyes' ability to capture light, from the simple nauplius eyes of the larval stages to the complex eyes of the adults, the same type of eyes that we find in insects and crustaceans today. Every nuance and every single lens is preserved, and it's clear that already during the Cambrian period, vision had nearly reached today's advanced levels.

THE EYE

Our human eye consists of a round, jelly-like vitreum. At one end, there's a lens suspended in muscle fibres, shaped to refract the rays of light and capture the surrounding reflection of photons both close up and on the horizon. Under the protection of the cornea lies the iris, named after the rainbow goddess of the same name. The iris controls the window to the world that is the pupil, the size of which varies according to the amount of light present. In the darkness of the night, the pupil dilates to receive all available light, while it grows smaller in the daylight. The iris not only directs the amount of light towards the retina and optic nerve but also communicates information. The impression we make on other people lies not to an insignificant degree in our eyes' unique colour combination, in its movements and in our exchanges of glances. The goddess Iris was the messenger between the gods and humanity, between the heavens and the earth. In the same way, our iris helps to interpret, and to convey our reactions to, the world around us.

When the light reaches the back portion of the vitreum, it's captured by the retina, where it is changed into electrical signals. The optic nerve sends a steady stream of data to the brain for interpretation. The light is then turned into images, images that we can summon even when we blink, that can come to life in dreams and be communicated through words. Through our eyes, we've captured our surroundings.

On the retina we find cones, colour-sensitive eye cells that sense blue, red, green and, in combination, all the nuances in our perceived colour spectrum. The more cones, the sharper the image. The three different types of cones we have give us access to all the colours of the rainbow but not to all the light. Birds have eyes that see more wavelengths, and just like we humans, they are visually directed animals. They rely almost completely on their good vision. But while we have to make do with three types of cones (three colours), birds have four. In addition to the three cones that are sensitive to blue, red and green, they have cones that respond to ultraviolet light. Furthermore, birds have oil droplets in their retinas. These work much like a camera filter on your smartphone, allowing shades of colours to be perceived even better. So, birds experience the world in a slightly different way than we do – we could argue that they experience a little more of it. But compared to the mantis shrimp, both birds and humans are put to shame. Mantis shrimp have up to sixteen different cones to perceive light waves, and their experience of colour is completely beyond our comprehension.

Human eyes are largely adapted for the daytime, and with the onset of darkness and the decreasing bombardment of photons through our growing pupils, our retinas change shape. Our cones, which need light to give definition and colour sensitivity, lose their ability to capture certain wavelengths. Details become blurred and colours fade. If a person has the patience on a dark evening without too much unnatural light, they can actually experience how their vision gets better and better. When dusk drains the world of colour, when there's not enough light for the cones, the work is taken over by the rods, the photoreceptor cells on the outer part of the retina. Rods are very light-sensitive but, unlike cones, give us no information about colour. Therefore, as the rods are activated, we see more and more details in the night, but we do so in greyscale.

The chemical process of capturing light has a long history, much longer than the eye with its ability to distinguish objects. We can actually trace it to before the Cambrian explosion, to *dinoflagellates*, single-celled algae that produced the protein rhodopsin. Translated from the Greek, 'rhodopsin' roughly means 'violet sight'. Rhodopsin is the light-sensitive substance that we find in the rods of the retina that allows us to see in low-light conditions, although not enabling us to distinguish between different colours. The gene that provides for our sight is found, strangely enough, in an organism that doesn't even belong to the animal kingdom.

Unlike humans, many animals are more adaptable to the light of night than to the shadows of day, including most mammals, whose visual sense has evolved for a life at dusk. Many have only two different types of cone and have instead adaptations to facilitate the capture of light by the rods. An example of such an enhancer is *tapetum lucidum* – an extra membrane that allows crepuscular light to pass over the retina twice for maximum harnessing of light. Who hasn't at some point seen a pair of cat eyes shining in the night? And what makes those eyes appear to shine is precisely their *tapetum lucidum*.

In the sprawling order of bats, megabats have their own family. The large, spectacular megabat species that can be seen flying at sunset in Africa, Asia and Oceania live on fruit or nectar, and unlike their smaller relatives, they use night vision rather than echolocation to orient themselves. Fruit bats' eyes have their own unique adaptation. They have lots of veins that cover the fundus behind the retina. The veins contain blood vessels that passively and continuously supply the retina with nutrition and oxygen without the retina itself needing any bulky blood vessels that would obscure and shade the rods. Before the discovery of echolocation (the ability most bats have to navigate in the dark using sound), most people thought, quite logically, that bats had almost supernatural night vision. That's why there are so many stories about how bats, and especially their blood, have been used to develop the ability to see in the blackest of nights. Chronicles of folklore from Broby, Skåne, from 1874 say: 'Coat the eyes with as much blood from a bat . . . as possible and you'll see as well at night as in the day.'

Bats' abilities would in this way be transferred to humans – and not just their night vision, either; bat blood was also alleged to cure eye injuries or to endow one's vison with philosophical clarity. That belief wasn't simply folklore but applied by learned people. One such person was Albertus Magnus or Albert the Great (c. 1200–80). He was a mediaeval theologian and naturalist, later to be canonised. Albertus Magnus was one of the first to interpret Aristotle's texts and had a great knowledge of the teachings of antiquity. It is said that he was fully convinced of the power of the bats, and that he was in the habit of rubbing his face each night with bat blood to endow himself with as good night vision as possible, so that he could continue reading books and parchment manuscripts well into the wee hours. Maybe he made use of this trick when he wrote his work *De animalibus* ('On Animals'), in which both dragons and unicorns occur, in keeping with mediaeval lore.

NOCTURNAL SENSES

When darkness settles over the meadows and the forests, shrews and hedgehogs hunt for their food. They sniff, wait, then walk carefully forwards. Mice and voles also dart past, gathering food. From the shadows, they are monitored by owls, who wait for the right time to strike. Their silent wings give an almost eerie impression out in the wilderness at night. There are about two hundred owl species in the world and the vast majority of these are loyal to the dark. When the usually solitary owls nest in the early spring, you can hear their characteristic 'hoo-ing' reclaiming the sunset or the coolest hours just before dawn. The mountain owl's desolate song sounds across the plains in the early evening, while the horned owl's fast, repetitive sounds belong to midnight. The female and the male stay together while the owlets mature, then go on different paths and return to their solitary lives.

In agrarian society, the owl was the friend of the farm. Each night, along with the farm cat, it kept voles, mice and young rats away from cereals and food stores. The rodents would otherwise multiply rapidly. The owl is often associated with mysticism and wisdom because it can find its way in the dark. Athena, the goddess of wisdom in Greek mythology, has an owl for a companion. But the owl's connection with darkness and all the unknown within it means that it's also surrounded by superstition. In particular, the tawny owl's plaintive cries were interpreted in earlier times as a bad omen and a harbinger of death.

The owl's large eyes have a hard time detecting details at close range. But they effectively capture the weakest of stray crepuscular light on their retinas, which are packed with photosensitive rods. At night, the owl can see a hundred times better than we humans. Its head can turn 270 degrees when it scouts and listens for clues, and the most nocturnal owls, such as the barn owl, have faces shaped like satellite dishes to be able to pick up even the faintest sounds from prey. Because its right and left ears are differently shaped, it's clear to an owl which direction the sounds are coming from. A delay of a microsecond between the sound hitting the right and then the left ear is enough for an owl to locate the slightest rustle with the utmost accuracy.

Another nocturnal and mythical bird is the European nightjar, with its drawn-out, buzzing, jarring sound that is a classic component of the Swedish summer night. From a distance, it may sound like a passing vehicle, but when you get closer you can identify the individual tones in the strange sound. If you catch the eye of the European nightjar in a light, it returns the gaze with large, ruby-red, shiny eyes. Its *tapetum lucidum*, the reflective membrane, makes its night vision very effective. The nightjar's scientific genus name *Caprimulgus* means goat-milker, which alludes to a very old belief about nightjars milking goats, during which they are harmed and eventually go blind. Maybe it was thought that the nightjar needed to rob other animals of their sight in order to see in the night itself.

In autumn, the nightjars migrate further south, just like so many other Nordic summer guests. And they follow a strict lunar calendar. When the full moon shines, they stop to eat because the light facilitates the capturing of insects. As the moonlight wanes, they fly ever-longer distances between their breaks.

In Sri Lanka, the owl is said to be the bat's consort, and in an older Swedish dialect, the nightjar and the bat can share the same name. All of them are animals that fly in the night, and up until the 1600s, bats were still considered birds. But while the nightjar relies on its good eyesight, and the owl on both sight and hearing, the bat has a sixth sense to find its way in the dark, namely echolocation.

In the eighteenth century, several zoologists were convinced that bats had particularly sensitive skin on their wings that allowed them to navigate in the dark, that they simply *felt* their way forwards. But in 1793, the Italian Lazzaro Spallanzani (1729–99) along with the Swiss Charles Jurine (1751–1819) showed that the ears were the bats' secret navigation instruments. After putting blindfolds on some bats and earplugs on others, they ascertained that only those with the blindfolds could fly through an obstacle course in darkness. The blinded bats could also capture insects, unlike the specimens deprived of hearing. Spallanzani and Jurine's experiments are preserved in a number of letters that they exchanged, but Spallanzani's dissertation on bats, titled *'Trattato dé Pipistrelli'*, was, for unknown reasons, never completed for publication. He was, however, widely known in scientific circles for his meticulous observations and studies of, among other things, the nightly movements of eels. It's been said that it was Spallanzani who gave E. T. A. Hoffmann (1776–1828) the inspiration for his short horror story 'The Sandman', about a scientist who constructs a female robot and in so doing drives a young man to madness.

Not until 1938 were researchers able to confirm that bats navigate with the aid of their hearing and that Spallanzani and Jurine were right. Harvard student Donald Griffin (1915–2003) had read a theory that bats could use high-frequency calls – sounds beyond human perception. These ideas had already been put forward after the First World War, when the defence industry was experimenting with sonar technology, the art of interpreting sound echoes. The theory had, however, never been tested in practice. Griffin contacted a physicist who designed an ultrasonic detector, an apparatus with which sounds above the frequency range perceptible by humans could be registered. Then he took a colleague and some bats with him into the physics lab. It didn't take long before they, for the first time, could hear the sound of the bat and together formulated the concept of echolocation.

Griffin died in 2003 and was active to the end. The previous year, he'd been at the North American Bat Conference, which is held every year in the days around Halloween. That year it was held in Burlington, Vermont, and the auditorium was filled to capacity when Griffin took the lectern. In bat circles, he's like Charles Darwin himself. After his lecture, it was hard to imagine that anyone would want to listen to me talk about bats' vision in a fifteen-minute summary of my upcoming dissertation (echolocation and all myths to the contrary, bats are not blind!). But Griffin sat in the front row and showed how curious he still was about bats, sixty-four years after his groundbreaking discovery.

Biosonar or *echolocation* means that with the help of sound and its echoes, different objects can be detected and located. Sound waves that bounce off of an object and return to their emitter can provide additional information regarding an object's distance and size, direction of movement and speed. And the shorter the wavelengths – that is to say the higher the tone used – the fewer objects the sound waves can reverberate against. We humans can use our voices to create an echo in a valley, but a bat can get tiny insects to reflect sound. And so they can catch their prey in total darkness.

The art of navigating and searching for food with the help of sound, in combination with flying ability, is the recipe for bats' success. But they aren't alone in this specialisation. Whales also use the same technique, albeit with low frequencies; so do cave-dwelling oilbirds (*guácharo*); and so do shrews, whose ears perceive ultrasound just like bats'. They can all navigate in the dark, whether it's in murky water, deep forests or cave systems or underneath the night sky. Echolocation and the ability to fly developed in tandem among the early bats in the prehistoric forests, between 60 million and 70 million years ago. Eventually, bats became experts at hunting nocturnal insects at a time when they could avoid speedy, diurnal predatory birds. Nighttime and darkness became an ecological niche in which they could find refuge from their natural enemies.

TWILIGHT ANIMALS

When reason sleeps, the monster awakens. Francisco de Goya's (1746–1828) famous work depicting a sleeping man bent over a table reveals the night to be a foreign world. Behind him looms darkness and dreams in the form of cats, owls and bats – the night's beloved, fantastical and feared animals.

But human beings aren't adapted for activities in the dark. Our senses are simply too limited, and moreover, our brains require a lot of sleep to be able to sort impressions and events. When the darkness of night falls, we usually become sleepy and withdraw. And when we save our Excel files in the late afternoon and turn off the lights in the office, or maybe even more commonly, just leave without turning them off, we begin a shift. The traffic jams are slowly rolling out of town, delivery vans are silent and the sun's rays are reddening. When the streetlights blink on, we know that it's evening and soon time for dinner, maybe a fair bit of time on the sofa and, after that, sleep. Individual night workers start their day, some nighttime hikers start moving, but in large part, people make a lot less fuss in the darkness.

Humans share their preference for daytime activity with the majority of primates, but otherwise, we're fairly unique among mammals. Most of the world's nearly six thousand species of mammals prefer the hours at dawn and dusk, or even the night, and have done so ever since the continents of the earth were fused in a single body of land and Europe was covered in tropical forest. While the dinosaurs were still around, early mammals moved under protection of darkness, with well-developed night vision, whiskers to feel around with, ears alert to the slightest rustle and a nose adapted to the scents of the night. Animals that sought refuge in darkness could escape predators and had the insect fauna of the night to eat. Many mammals were initially small and lived in trees, shrubs or on the ground under the protection of fallen leaves. They sustained themselves mainly on seeds, insects and other small animals. Only when the sun was setting did they venture out in search of food. From these proto-mammals evolved the genetic basis for everything from large land predators to whales to bats, all the fauna we see around us today. And they were all born in the shadows. When the dinosaurs eventually died out, the mammals took over the vacant niches, spread out, grew and even ventured into the daylight. But our dogs still find scent traces more easily in the evening moisture, and it's during my twilight trips in search of bats that I see moose crossing the road, marten eyes glistening from the edge of the forest and foxes hunting in the fields. Mammals are still largely twilight animals that are least active in the middle of the day. Even animals that we associate with daytime activity, such as certain squirrels, ungulates and most carnivorans, have some of the characteristic night senses left.

Cat owners are not infrequently woken up by their cat meowing and wanting to go out in the middle of the night. At home, the cat may be timid and lazy, but outdoors it's still wild. In 2013, the BBC documentary *The Secret Life of the Cat* was broadcast. The documentary was based on studies of fifty cats in a residential area in the UK. Each cat had been equipped with GPS and a micro-camera, and every movement was documented. It turned out that all cats had well-defined home ranges and that those were smaller than previously thought. Several cats were able to divide a given area, and they patrolled at different times, some at night, some during the day. Some were decidedly twilight animals, others made use of the entire day. It wasn't uncommon for cats to enter other cats' homes and eat their food. When they were discovered, a power struggle ensued.

With the help of modern night cameras that can operate in very low light, it's been possible in recent years to see that more animals are active at night than we previously knew. Cheetahs, for example, which normally hunt during the day, use the light of the full moon on the plains to take almost as much prey under the moonlight.

Elephants have always been most active during daylight on the savannah, even though matriarchs sometimes lead their herds to waterholes when the night's beneficial coolness has descended. Moving in the dark gives nocturnal hunters such as lions and hyenas the advantage, but despite this, several African elephant herds have begun to show more and more activity at dusk in recent years. The reason is poachers. The darkness of night protects the elephants from poachers, and it has been shown that the oldest members of the herd are well aware of the reserve boundaries, where they can go safely and where they are exposed to stalking by humans. Only under cover of darkness do the elephants move between two nature reserves.

In desert areas around the world, the sun's rays are so hot that they kill, which is why night is a sanctuary for all living things, including cacti that bloom only in the dark in anticipation of the bats' pollination trips. Mongooses are catlike predators that live on the savannah and are close relatives of the meerkat. Mongooses have always been considered a typical daytime mammal, but two researchers decided to take a closer look at what they do at night. Not surprisingly, they turned out to have a relatively active night life. Several individuals changed their residence, one chased away an intruder, another examined holes in a different area. The mongooses didn't lie down and sleep through the nights; they had interactions both inside their dug cavities and out in the night air.

Life has evolved in accordance with the day's alternating light and darkness, and the more animals we study, the more we realise that day and night are equally important for their ecology. In an increasingly illuminated world, the boundaries of the day are blurred and activity patterns change. We still know very little about what this actually means for animal and plant life.

SING IN THE WRONG LIGHT

One of the most familiar sounds of the night, especially at southern latitudes, is the persistent, high-frequency chirping of crickets and frogs. Many people find the sounds soothing; there are soundtracks that play the sound of crickets for people who want to shut out other noise and possibly fall asleep more easily. But in some cases, their frequency is right on the edge of what we can perceive, and those sounds can be experienced as extremely unpleasant.

Their sounds are used both for marking territory and as a mating song. The male most often plays his serenades in the evening. The cricket's song is linked to the transition between light and darkness, and small changes in the intensity of the light are enough for the cricket to put off its song and miss the timing of the mating ritual. Females and males risk not meeting at night as they should. In addition, if the light is too bright, the growth of the young crickets, the nymphs, is delayed. It's precisely the length of the day that tells the insects what time of year it is, so that they can speed up or slow down their growth based on the amount of light available.

The song of the crickets attracts attention, not only from the opposite sex but also from predators. Those crickets singing in the wrong light run an extra-high risk of becoming food before they've had time to mate, a problem that crickets share with many insects. Moths around lights and lamp-posts after dawn are easy prey. It has been shown that birds, as well as rats, lizards, toads and spiders, take advantage of the fact that insects gather and remain near lights. These advantaged predators have a buffet already laid out for them. Even while it's still dark and the moths are fluttering around the streetlights, they're already easy targets. At that time, the bats are the enemy more than anything else.

My colleagues in the small bat group at the University of Gothenburg studied interactions between moths and bats in Gothenburg at the turn of the twentieth century, with the help of, among other things, a small ultrasonic generator that could emit high-frequency sounds just like a bat makes. With it in hand, you could make moths react in different ways. As though following signals from a remote control, a selected moth was made to dive to the ground, turn on a dime or do a loop in the night's darkness. One push of a button and their wings stopped beating, another and they turned off course to confuse any pursuers. When a bat sends out its echolocation sounds in search of prey, they can do so at up to 130 decibels. So, a prey animal that hears high frequencies has no problem picking up the sounds of bats. Having developed just such a defence, moths can normally avoid being sitting ducks for hungry hunters at night.

When the ultrasonic generator was tested on moths under streetlamps instead, however, they were seemingly deaf and had no reaction whatsoever. Under the lights, they didn't hear the high-frequency sounds. It seems that light simply distracts from their natural auditory system. The explanation is that moths react differently to dangers depending on whether it's light or dark. Birds are the main threat during the day and bats at night. The results, which were first published in the scientific journal

Animal Behaviour in 1998, have been cited many times in recent years, for they fit perfectly into the new field of light pollution study.

The eyes of nocturnal insects are particularly sensitive to green, blue and ultraviolet, and it's these wavelengths more than any others that motivate them to fly towards lights. So, orange streetlamps, which are the most common along our roads, attract fewer insects than the older white lamps (mercury lamps), which all emitted a large amount of light in shades of violet. The clouds of insects that could previously be collected about 50 metres around each lamp-post can no longer be seen at the same levels. But as a trade-off, there are more lights.

Moreover, today there's a plethora of different kinds of lights, all with different wavelengths, all with different levels of draw for insects. A standard streetlight attracts insects from a distance of about 20 metres, but sometimes it's up to 50. Given that streetlights are usually closer together than that, it's extremely difficult for insects to cross a road without being ensnared by a light source. This means that every road, even the smallest pavement, acts as a kind of a barrier.

Even if we were to stick to amber or even red lights, which insects can to some extent ignore, or we managed to design lights with well-defined spectrums so as not to disturb the insects' orientation, the intensive use of artificial light would still mean that we were always spilling light out into the sky. A light without a shade radiates more light and energy into the atmosphere than onto the walkway it was intended to illuminate. And all this waste becomes a field of diffuse light – so-called *skyglow*. On a cloudy evening when the light is reflected back to earth, skyglow can cover our cities with a yellow dome and completely block out the night sky, and in that light insects have still other problems.

The light of the full moon can be bright enough to keep

certain insect species staying on the ground, as they could otherwise be easily taken by predators. They would rather wait for darker nights than fly under the moon and risk their lives. Normally, this isn't a problem. As is well known, the moon travels its silent path, and soon the darkness is back. The phases of the moon are predictable and recurring, constituting one of the cycles in nature that can affect and calibrate the biological clock. Sometimes, however, a cloud in front of a partial moon is enough for the insects to take wing and go out into the night. But under a constantly artificially lit sky, even if it seems dark to our eyes, it's as if the full moon is always present and often even brighter than that. Under such a sky, not even the clouds are helpful; quite the contrary, as they reflect the light back towards the earth.

NATURE'S OWN LANTERNS

Patterns and warning colours that on animals and insects are meant to camouflage, scare, deceive, entice or communicate toxicity to others were developed over the course of millions of years to be most effective at a particular time of day. When we turn on a source of light, colours are reflected differently, patterns become distorted and shapes are blurred. All our different types of lights – from decorative garden lanterns to facade lighting – glow in different ways, casting different nuances and wavelengths into the night. While colour contrasts are enhanced in one kind of light, they are diminished in another kind of light. Instead of being hidden in the dark, a creature could suddenly be fully visible. Instead of attracting a partner, it could be discovered by a predator.

There are kinds of moths that do everything they can to be seen during twilight, and this endeavour gives rise to a grand spectacle recurring each year. In Sweden, ghost moths are large, chalk-white moths that cannot hear, and they fly over unmown meadows in the pale, washed-out darkness of a June night. Just as the fog drifts off streams and cairns, and the woodcock takes its last tour of the evening, the first ghost moths appear. They take their place in the meadow and quietly start rising, like they are using an invisible lift. Up and down, up and down, in a tireless, rhythmic movement. Soon, others follow suit, and before you know it, the meadow is a sea of bobbing silver-white moths. They're all males who've shown up in hopes of finding a female. Their mating dance takes place in the same place, at the same time, every year, and their white wings are clearly visible against the dark green grass in the dwindling evening light. But the ghost moths are playing a dangerous game. It doesn't take long before a northern bat dives down from its patrolling height of 4 metres above the ground, makes an elegant U-turn and catches a moth just above the tops of the blades of grass. Several times I've witnessed both the ghost moths' flirtatious dance to ensure the next generation, and how the northern bats materialise from the shadows behind the tree curtains to immediately plunge down into the swaying grass. After about forty-five minutes, everything suddenly stops. The meadow's silver-white wave subsides, the bats move on and an owl hoots that the evening's show is over. Midsummer twilight has passed and with it the shortened night. Dawn is rising again.

In a recent year, I witnessed a lone ghost moth in an overgrown ditch as he rode his invisible lift in the summer night. Otherwise, it's been a long time since I've seen them dancing over the countryside in the evening. Twilight is chased off by artificial light, large-scale agriculture is taking over, and the old meadows become planted over. The moth populations are dwindling.

We know that the ghost moths fly at a time when the natural light best reflects off their white wings; that's how the males gain the females' attention. In artificial light, the contrast between the light colour of their wings and the evening sky is masked and the mating dance fades out, literally. No one has done a formal study on the effects of this, not on the ghost moths in Sweden. But other species have been found to be affected in a similar way – species that also turn up in the dark with spectacular signals. A clear example are the glow-worms, those beetles that have built-in lanterns and glow with a bright yellow-green shine in summer meadows and clearings such as here in Sweden. The females lack cover wings and look a bit like caterpillars, which is why they are inaccurately called 'worms'. At dusk, she climbs out on a leaf or a blade of grass, directs her glowing backside towards the sky and waits. Soon, males come flying, lured by the seductive light, which looks like a small diode in the night. The males also glow, but only mildly, not as phosphorescently green as the females.

In some places, glow-worms are present in such large numbers that they've become tourist attractions. One such place is Waitomo in New Zealand, where half a million visitors descend each year into a bustling underground labyrinthian cave to be greeted by a ghostly glow from above. Hundreds of thousands of glow-worms give off a bluish light, like the glitter of the moon across a rippling sea. The glow-worms are of a different variety than those in the Nordic countries; they are mosquito larvae, which, after they have hatched on the brink of spring, spin a small nest of silk thread. From each of the thousands of small settlements, about twenty long threads hang, each outfitted with sticky drops reflecting light in all directions and creating a tapestry of pulsating wonder over the ceiling of the cave. The threads catch gnats and other small insects attracted by the larvae's built-in diodes. The larvae are sometimes called spider worms precisely because of their ability to spin threads and trap prey in the way that spiders do. The adult mosquitoes also glow. Why isn't known for certain, but it could, of course, have to do with mating. This is really the only task adult individuals have. When they have found a partner and the female has placed her eggs on the cave walls, they die, only to make room for a new generation of luminescent larvae.

In Tasmania, there's another cave with glowing creatures of the same genus. They shine just as seductively and attract visitors from near and far. The light of the larvae appears dimmed and faded in brighter conditions, which is why the tourism industry does its best to completely avoid artificial light. In addition, the display is best experienced with eyes that are as adapted to the darkness as possible. I myself have walked in a New Zealand forest before dawn, guided only by thousands of glow-worms in the vegetation of the bush, as though in the wake of a fire-breathing dragon. They gave off so much light that not once during my 5-kilometre promenade did I have to turn on my torch. But in a commercial context, lighting still needs to be used. In the Tasmanian cave, the effects of the lights that help tourists see where they set foot have been studied, and it actually seems like the insects handle it pretty well. They recover quickly, and their natural rhythm continues along its normal course, as long as the lights aren't on for too long or too often. But that's the case for mosquito larvae in caves, where it gets really dark, where the effect of a light disappears quickly. It's worse for the glow-worms in Europe, the beetles that crawl up on grass blades in the open air. Their light is turned on after sunset and is strongest and most effective just before the first hour of dawn, while the darkness is still thick.

In England, the public has been reporting discoveries of glow-worms since 1990, at a time when it was feared that the dramatic creatures were disappearing. And even though the number of sites where they were found increased at first, you can now see a negative trend – the glow-worms *are* disappearing. The ones that are found are mainly now in nature reserves and in the countryside, far from the light of the cities.

The females wait out the day in a hiding place and turn on their lights shortly into the early twilight. Under an artificially lit sky, her light will stay off, despite the fact that her inner clock has aroused her desire to mate. Even if she climbs out on the blade of grass with her light on, there's no guarantee that it will be visible.

Females' signals are drowned out in all the surrounding light, and even light the equivalent strength of the full moon's is enough to reduce the males' accuracy. At the same time, the males may react to other lights shining from afar, going towards them in the hope of finding a large colony of females. In many cases, they fly far away, deceived by stray lights from windows, cars or streetlamps.

Unlike the green lights of the glow-worms, fireflies produce a yellower light. Fireflies can be found mostly in warmer areas; they flash in yellow, amber, orange and green, communicating with each other with a method that can be compared to Morse code. In Chinese mythology, fireflies appear when the grass of the plains is on fire, and in Japan they symbolise the light of human souls from the past. They fascinate and attract us, and in several parts of the world there are stories about how children used to collect fireflies in jars to use as lights at night, but today those are mostly tales to tell the grandchildren. Just as in the case of the glow-worm, the name is misleading. The firefly is also a beetle, and the fact is that glow-worms and fireflies can, in some cases, refer to the same beetle species, in which the female is stationary, glowing, while the male flies. When the male in the mating dance flashes his light, the female responds by flashing back. The two create an alliance and glow together in confirmation. The light can also guide them in the hunt for food in the dark and scare predators by signalling that the firefly is poisonous. In some places, entire colonies of fireflies can be seen flashing in sync, like a pulsating control panel, during dark tropical nights. One such place is the mangrove swamp in the Philippines, where female fireflies sit in the trees, blinking light green, while the males fly above the trees blinking back, all together, as if it were a surreal, extraterrestrial Christmas show. It's no wonder that myths arise about fireflies as fleeing souls and about how they can show lost travellers the way home.

LIGHT SPRING

The American author and marine biologist Rachel Carson (1907–64) is one of the environmental movement's paramount early figures. Her book *Silent Spring*, which came out in 1962, criticised the widespread use of the insecticide DDT and foresaw the insect die-off we are seeing today. Without insects, there are no birds and no birdsong. *Silent Spring* is about nothing less than the dystopian silence of an impoverished ecosystem. Sweden was the first country to ban DDT in 1969, and the rest of the world was soon to follow suit. Although it hasn't got quite so bad that the spring has gone silent, insect-eating birds are following the same trend as their prey and are in decline. For other birds, especially omnivores that can find food in cities, things are improving instead.

One urban bird, the European blackbird, has, with its recognisable melodic trilling, been named Sweden's national bird. It was once known as a forest bird with a preference for the deep, dark woods. It was somewhat shy and settled among thickets in humid, shady environments. Its dark plumage blended into the foliage as it searched for food in the soil, hiding its exact position among branches and leaves, singing its songs. But in tandem with industrialisation in the nineteenth century, the blackbird became part of the city. Fewer and fewer blackbirds bothered migrating in the winter, and those that stayed sang louder and longer into the autumn. In noisy metropolitan environments, they also sang louder simply to be heard over the traffic.

In the mediaeval city of Leipzig in Germany, project researchers spent their evenings studying the behaviour of the blackbird. More than anything, they wanted to investigate how long after sunset the birds continued to hunt and eat, and to compare results from forest and park environments to those from the city centre. It turned out that the brighter the lights of the city, the later in the evening the blackbirds were active. Kind of like humans. It was especially clear on the edge of spring.

Sometimes on my way home from bat studies in the field in the wee hours of the morning, I hear songbirds already up at two o'clock, long before dawn has any plans to show up. In fact, light equivalent to that of the full moon is enough to trigger the songs of some birds, especially in the spring when they're establishing their mating territories. A male who's out early naturally has a greater chance of impressing females with his persistent songs.

In Munich, just over 350 kilometres south of the Leipzig bird route, other blackbirds have shown researchers how much light they're actually exposed to on a daily basis. The birds have been equipped with small light recorders that measure the amount of incoming light around the clock, storing the information on a chip. In this way, it has been found that urban populations of blackbirds are, on average, exposed to just over a thousand times more light at night than forest populations of the same species. While forest blackbirds live in light conditions that roughly correspond to cloudy autumn nights, urban blackbirds always have at least a full moon's worth of light. Additionally, they get almost an hour longer of the daylight experience.

In 2019, more blackbirds singing into autumn were reported than ever before, especially in the Stockholm area. The mild

November weather, combined with the city lights, seems to have given the birds a sense of spring. The normal shadow song, the quiet growl that you can hear from them in the winter, had suddenly been replaced by a trilling mating song in the middle of the November darkness. People often react strongly to the song of the blackbirds, and maybe this isn't so strange. We've been influenced by the sound since we took our first steps, and their song is so intimately associated with spring that their spring feelings spread to us. We instinctively feel that it sounds wrong to hear blackbird song accompanied by Christmas music in the city shops.

Urban birds have habits extending both earlier and later in the seasons than their cospecies in forest environments, and they also have a longer mating season. They have more time to sing, socialise and find food. In some cases, the city birds have almost a month longer to have their young, because they reach sexual maturity earlier. They might even manage to have several broods in a single season. In addition to the increased day length – even if it's artificial – it's also warmer in the city, and there are often fewer predators there. But still it's not a given that the city birds feel better; in fact, the extended length of day doesn't seem to give them the long-term physical benefits that one might expect.

One reason is that the birds' hormonal systems are impacted. The return of sunlight in the spring is supposed to initiate the desire to mate, sing and produce sex cells. It's after the long winter nights, during longer days with higher temperatures, that the eggs are to be laid and, eventually, when the insects have come back to life and the summer smorgasbord has been set, the chicks are supposed to hatch. Light-sensitive receptors in both the hypothalamus and the pineal gland help constantly to adjust the hereditary internal clock to optimise for the survival of the next generation of birds. But when the light is deceptive and obscures the arrival of spring and the length of nighttime, birds become sexually mature at the wrong time. In the best case, it gives the birds a competitive advantage; in the worst case, the timing between males and females is off, eggs hatch before there's food to be had and the body's systems are under stress. A study in Florida showed that sparrows infected with West Nile fever, a viral disease related to yellow fever and hepatitis C, had an average of two days more infection time if they were exposed to artificial light during that time. So, the lighting in the cities had an inhibitory effect on the birds' immune systems, which also increases the risk of the virus spreading to humans.

With bats and deer, mating takes place in the autumn, and they obviously don't want to have their offspring in the middle of winter. The female bat therefore stores semen until the spring weather shows that it's time for the egg to be fertilised. This also allows the mating season to be extended into the winter, energy permitting. In contrast, the female deer's eggs are fertilised directly, but foetal development doesn't start until after the turn of the year, so that the fawn isn't born prematurely. Adaptations like these are governed by several factors, in which the length of the day is an important piece of the puzzle.

In southwestern Australia, there lives a small, kangaroo-like animal, the tammar wallaby. Tammar wallabies give birth to their young six weeks after the summer solstice. Then, they ensure that the female has the greatest access to food and can produce as much milk as possible when the young need it most. The signal to start the process is a change in the light, which, like a calendar, gives word when the time is right. But in a population of tammar wallabies in the villages of Garden Island off the coast of Australia, it was recently noticed that the young were being born later, up to a month after the usual time. This turned out to be due to the proximity of a naval base that cast its spotlight over their territory. The artificial light obscured the natural cycles with the wrong wavelengths of light, distorting the calendar of the evening sky. Hormone systems were disrupted, and the whole process, from mating to birth and growth, was delayed. The wallabies weren't born until that season's food had already begun to run out. Nature was again disrupted by man-made light.

THE STAR COMPASS

In Sweden, we have an incredible diversity of birds during the summer, when food is most available. But when darkness steadily returns and the temperature drops, hordes of birds head south. They travel from the uninterrupted light of the polar summer to the regular cycles of light and darkness in the tropics. All over the earth, birds move between winter and summer places and between rainy and dry seasons to nest where the food is. The Arctic tern travels 40,000 kilometres a year; that is a whole trip around the earth.

To find the same place year after year, birds have a whole host of tools at their disposal, such as an extraordinary memory for landmarks and the ability to navigate by the sun. They can also sense and read the earth's magnetic field and so determine how far north or south they are – they have an inner compass. How this works has been the subject of much research. Particles of the magnetic substance magnetite have been found in birds, which could be part of the explanation, but there are many indications that they actually use their eyes. In a ring around the edge of the retina are cryptochromes – proteins that are particularly sensitive to blue light. The cryptochromes are found in both animals and plants and are involved in, among other things, governing the circadian rhythm. But a type of cryptochrome protein has also been shown to respond to magnetic fields. Maybe it's the case that birds and other animals, too, can simply see the earth's magnetic field.

To be able to travel several hundred kilometres and find their way back to the same place year after year, birds also use other nocturnal clues. In fact, nocturnal migrations are very common, especially for small birds. It is estimated that two-thirds of all migratory birds make their long-haul flights at night. In the 1950s, the ornithologist couple Eleanor and Franz Sauer built a glass cage that they took turns sitting in during the evenings. They had also placed warblers in the cage, which during the migration period showed clear signs of wanting to flee into the night. On starry nights, the birds made outbursts in a given direction, while on cloudy evenings they were somewhat calmer, more tentative, and not as clear that they wanted to go. The husband and wife wanted to test the hypothesis that birds can navigate by the stars, so they constructed their own planetarium with each star depicted as a small point of light in the ceiling. They moved the warblers in there. The projection of the starry sky in the planetarium could be turned on and off and rotated, and it showed that as long as everything was normal, as long as the stars shone brightly in the dark blue-painted ceiling, all the warblers headed in the same direction every night. If the starry sky was put out, though, there was confusion in the flock and the birds tried to head off in slightly different directions, if they tried at all. Several of them just sat down and preened their feathers, apparently in anticipation of better weather. The most interesting discovery made by the Sauer couple was that it was possible to influence the birds' perception of which direction was right simply by turning the projection. It was quite obvious that the birds were studying the starry sky and acting according to its pattern. The question was how.

If there's a single star that most of us living in the northern hemisphere know by sight, it's the North Star. At a distance of nearly 300 light-years away, it's clearly visible as a constant guide in an otherwise changing night sky. Around the North Star, the Plough and the entire starry sky rotates slowly anti-clockwise as the night progresses. The North Star is the celestial pole, the celestial vault's equivalent to the geographic North Pole. The phenomenon has guided seafarers through all ages and probably also birds. Stephen T. Emlen wanted to find out if that was the case, so he picked up where Franz and Eleanor Sauer left off. Emlen chose to work with indigo buntings, beautiful blue cardinals that move between North America and the Caribbean every year. He created a system whereby the birds tramped around in ink so every movement, every launch in a certain direction, made small footprints on a piece of paper. Emlen's research involved the birds' circadian rhythm and what they saw in thc sky. By carefully blocking out selected parts of the constellations in his manufactured starry sky, he would eventually come to the conclusion that the North Star and the Plough were the starting point for their navigation.

But Emlen didn't stop there; he also made the homemade night sky rotate around another star instead. He moved the celestial pole to Betelgeuse, a bright, red giant star in the constellation Orion, known to anyone who has read Douglas Adams' classic *The Hitchhiker's Guide to the Galaxy*. Betelgeuse has consumed all its hydrogen, so it glows red instead of white, and it is expected to flare up into a supernova at any time. It could happen today or in a thousand years, and when it happens, we'll be able to see the spectacle with our naked eyes, even during the day. Otherwise, it's in the December darkness that Betelgeuse can be most clearly seen on one of Orion's shoulders. When Emlen's indigo buntings saw that the sky was spinning around Betelgeuse instead of around the North Star, they aimed for it to try and start their journey north. Another group of birds, which Emlen had tricked into thinking it was autumn, tried to fly in the exact opposite direction. Emlen's and Sauer's experiments have been repeated many times in the last fifty years in many different ways, and it seems as if birds have an innate ability to recognise the pattern of the stars closest to the celestial poles. This knowledge, together with their inner compass, leads them the right way on their long, nocturnal journeys across the earth.

It's long been known that night-travelling birds fly high when the moon shines in a clear sky and the stars can be counted in their thousands. On cloudy nights, rain and fog make the birds fly lower. At such times, there's an imminent risk that the large flocks will be confused by lights and buildings, and there are many recorded observations of birds that have collided in large numbers with masts, towers and lighthouses around the world. A notorious incident occurred in 1968 when no less than five thousand birds, mostly songbirds, collided with a television tower in Nashville, USA. And below the lighthouse at Long Point in southern Canada, a total of seven thousand dead or injured individuals were found between 1960 and 1969. In fact, as early as 1880, a compilation of birds that died at lighthouses in North America was made: the lighthouses off the east and south coasts – in Louisiana, Florida and North and South Carolina – were the most dangerous places and coincided with some of the most important migration routes.

Knowledge about the mesmerising attraction of light has been used as a hunting method by people in several parts of the world. In India, it was reported in the early twentieth century that birds could easily be caught if lanterns were lit during nights when the fog was thick and the wind came from the south. On the African savannah, in modern times it has been made a tourist attraction to lure birds in the twilight with mobile spotlights for viewing by visitors. As early as 1883, before the breakthrough of electric light, Darwin's friend and younger colleague George John Romanes (whom I talked about in the chapter 'The Vacuum Cleaner Effect'), likened the attraction of light for birds to that for moths. He wondered if a burning candle flame, an unusual phenomenon in nature, could be mistaken for a white flower or other objects that stimulated their innate curiosity. He also noted a similar behaviour in fish attracted to lanterns hung off of boats, a fact known by fishermen since time immemorial. Whether insects, birds or fish, darkness is essential to all living creatures.

THE DAZZLING CITY

On 11 September each year, the art installation *Tribute in Light* is lit in New York, where the Twin Towers once stood. The installation consists of eighty-eight spotlights that together create two shimmering blue pillars of light. On a clear night, they reach 6 kilometres into the atmosphere and can be seen from 100 kilometres away, despite the big city's other lights. The annual tribute to the victims of the terrorist attacks is witnessed and appreciated by tens of thousands of people, but it also coincides with the migrations of birds flying past the city. Because the spotlights are only lit one night each year, they are an excellent opportunity for researchers to study the effects of light. Between 2010 and 2017, the birds' reactions to and flight patterns around the somewhat extraterrestrial pillars were studied, and researchers found a number of strange behaviours. Shortly after the lights were lit, large flocks of birds gathered near them and flew around in circles, chirping and twittering. Just over one million birds were estimated to have assembled on the seven occasions that *Tribute in Light* was lit during the course of the study. However, as soon as the lights turned off, the flocks dispersed again. The study clearly showed that light affects and confuses birds. As skyscrapers grew high on North America, the problem of light-confused birds only increased. The lights and the skyglow that big cities cause blur out the stars even on clear nights and lure birds down from their normal altitude.

And given how the world's big cities are expanding and spreading their light further and further into the countryside, and higher into the atmosphere, the nights are increasingly rarely starry enough for navigation. Once among the skyscrapers and towers, the birds get stuck in the maze of confusing lights, reflective glass and tall obstacles. Strong lights can have a mesmerising effect on birds, and sometimes they get caught in the cones of light like confused moths. From a distance, the city centre light can also resemble the streak of the horizon, which is why birds retreat there or go completely off course. It can also be as simple as the light preventing the birds' natural night vision, even dazzling them, so that they have to take themselves down towards the ground to look for landmarks.

The Great Salt Lake in Utah is North America's richest bird sanctuary. Here, you can count the number of birds passing through in the millions every year. Beach and sea birds, waders, birds just taking breaks and nesting pairs from more than three hundred species coexist in the salt lake and its surrounding wetlands. You could say that the Great Salt Lake is North America's answer to Lake Hornborga, although it's a smaller inland sea rather than a lake. Southeast of the Great Salt Lake, Salt Lake City is growing. Even if it's a relatively small town by North American standards, it still has 200,000 inhabitants and hosted the Winter Olympic Games in 2002. Once an important mining community and the Mormons' refuge from persecution, the urban region is growing rapidly along the eastern parts of the salt lake towards the towns of Ogden and Logan, and the lights from residential suburbs and city centres get reflected by the salty, nutrient-rich wetlands, colouring the sky a pale orange. Salt Lake City residents are beginning to understand the seriousness of the threat to the mighty diversity of birds that live and thrive in the area. Since 2014, Tracy Aviary, a botanical garden and a centre for bird research in the city centre, has been working to educate the public and organise public research into light pollution. Residents of all ages have joined in to count the dead birds in the mornings in the centre of Salt Lake City, where each participant follows an assigned route. It also maps 'unnecessary light', such as decorative facade lighting and lights that are badly shaded or blindingly bright.

Tracy Aviary has also initiated a movement whereby any resident can sign an affidavit pledging to turn off their garden lights and dim their window lights during the birds' migration seasons, which run from March to May and from August to October. Participants must fill in a form stating that they are working actively to counteract light pollution, and then they get a sign to put on their house that shows three birds against a black, stylised silhouette of high-rise buildings, with the Rocky Mountains towering in the background. More precisely, it's the Wasatch Range, which constitutes the western outpost of the Rocky Mountains. The mighty range should remain dark at night, Tracy Aviary maintains, so that the natural light contrast between the distant, shadowy mountain peaks and the pale salt deposits on the fields in the valleys below can be preserved for future generations.

FALSE SUMMER

One late-autumn afternoon a couple of years ago, I was walking through Gothenburg, Sweden. The cafés projected autumn cosiness and beckoned with coffee and buns. The Halloween signs had been taken down, and here and there Advent candle holders had been put up far too soon. It was tempting to grab a seat with a blanket and a hot drink and fall into temporary slumber, but I continued my walk. Most of the trees had recently shed their leaves, but here and there, colourful birches and maples were lit by spotlights from below. In the light, the trees still had all their autumn splendour, all their clothes on. From a human perspective, it was actually quite beautiful. But it still felt wrong.

Plants capture sunlight with the help of chlorophyll, a pigment found in the chloroplasts of plant cells. The green light is reflected and gives the leaves their perceived colour. Newly sprouted leaves are light green and filter the spring sunlight on its way to the ground, and everything that's budding has its start there. Soon, they darken to the green hue characteristic of summer. In the autumn, when the light fades and the days are compressed, chlorophyll disappears and the leaves change their range of colour to be all shades of fire, before they eventually let go. The trees are ready for the winter cold.

Just like the warmer weather, the glow of lights can deceive the organism, and the falling leaves are delayed, remaining on the trees until well into late autumn. On the continent, botanists have seen how rowan and maple trees next to streetlamps remain with leaf cover for three whole weeks longer than their cospecies that are allowed to grow in natural light, despite being in a similar climate.

At the start of spring, artificial light can accelerate the awakening of the trees, making the buds open prematurely. Their rest is cut short; larger trees like oaks and beeches can bloom about a week earlier when exposed to street light, while smaller plants are more sensitive and can be triggered to bud even earlier in the late winter. So, while the darker forests of the countryside are still asleep, the city's plant life is ready for the summer even before the frost has let go, as if the stress of city life has sunk its claws even into the plant kingdom.

Each plant has its own adaptation as to what time of the season to flower to maximise its number of seeds. Releasing their seeds early and gaining a foothold in the field before their competitors can be an advantage, but spring can also be treacherous. When the cold strikes, newly sprouted buds are very sensitive, which is why the plants need to be able to rely on guidance from the environment. Apple trees are one example; their flower buds freeze off during a spring frost, a phenomenon many growers have experienced with increasing frequency. Temperature, number of hours of sunshine and the colour nuances of light all provide the clues to the right time. Global warming and artificial light together can therefore create major problems within plant ecosystems.

It was a poet and visual artist who first studied plants' reaction to different light wavelengths. Robert Hunt (1807–87) was educated in physics, chemistry and anatomy and was a promising writer and poet. Like so many of the former pioneers within science, he was a multitasker, with one foot in art, the other in the search for knowledge. Hunt's life was largely influenced by photography. The camera was new in his youth and he realised the possibilities and power of this new medium. With his knowledge of chemistry, he experimented with the development process, and with his knowledge of physics, he studied light itself and its wavelengths.

In the 1840s, Hunt discovered that different parts of the light spectrum affected plants in different ways. The shorter wavelengths of sunlight, the blue and violet light, are usually the ones signalling to seeds to germinate, while redder light with longer wavelengths normally initiates the flowering phase. It wasn't until the twentieth century that what controls this process was identified, when the various plant pigments, the *phytochromes*, were discovered. These are proteins that assume different shapes depending on ambient light conditions. Phytochromes are simply reshaped when light changes, a process that takes place at lightning speed and makes the plants perceive differences between wavelengths – the colours of light.

How the plants react depends on the context in which they live. Different lights have different properties, and plants react to both intensity and colour. Many modern lights (LED lights) glow white, almost bluish, resembling the morning sun's mix of short and long wavelengths. Older light bulbs, like in streetlights, are often yellow or amber in colour and more similar to the late-afternoon sky, which is dominated by longer wavelengths. This light has sometimes been shown to inhibit, rather than accelerate, the flowering of certain plants. In England, researchers have studied meadows in Cornwall, in particular the bird's-foot trefoil, a plant that we recognise by its characteristically shaped yellow flowers on midsummer meadows and heaths. Normally, they attract large numbers of aphids, but a late flowering or the absence of flowering can decimate entire populations of aphids, which in turn affects green lacewings, damselflies, ladybirds, hoverflies and the same insects we're used to seeing flying over the meadows that live on flowers and aphids. The domino effect begins, and the ecosystem is disrupted.

FRUITLESS NIGHT

In September of 2017, a mysterious glow was reported over Härnösand, Sweden. Had a UFO landed? The local media took photos as well as testimonials from curious residents. But it wasn't a UFO. The low clouds of the dark evening were reflecting light from a newly opened greenhouse. We humans can trick plants into serving us. Greenhouses with round-the-clock lighting do just that. The natural time for flowering and seeding may not suit us and so we can force a desired course of action by providing the plants with more or less light based on our demands, not their needs.

Every year, I get a poinsettia from my mother. It adorns the kitchen table for a while, but after it has bloomed, no one expects it to bloom again. In Mexico, where the poinsettia actually belongs, it has a longer flowering period, which depends on the length of the day or, really, the length of the night. The poinsettia is a so-called short-day plant, needing just over half a day in uninterrupted darkness in combination with the right temperature to bloom. To sell the red poinsettia at Christmas every year, the plants must be prepared in October. In greenhouses, the light is set to trick the plants to think that they're growing under the Mexican night sky.

Nearly all plants require darkness; their light-sensitive phytochromes react to the alternations between light and darkness, and the length of the night largely determines what they should be doing when it comes to resting or growing. For the short-day plant, the darkness is more crucial and it might more appropriately be called the long-night plant. The darkness needs to be consistent, creating an uninterrupted rest from the influence of light. During the course of evolution, perfect timing was coded into these genes to give the plant maximum opportunity to spread their seeds and thus their genes to the next generation.

We humans can take advantage of this. Had I been a little more enterprising with my poinsettia, after the Christmas flowering period I could have placed it in a dark cupboard for thirteen hours a day and in a bright window for eleven. The plant would then have been triggered to bloom again and again.

The alternative to short-day growth is of course long-day growth. These plants need a short night, or a short period of uninterrupted darkness followed by a longer, bright day, which is typical of our Swedish summer. Greenhouses around the world incorporate this fact, and it's not uncommon to see the lights on around the clock. Global warming and artificial light reset the internal clocks of the plants, risking destroying the delicate balance between plant and pollinator, between plant and herbivore, between prey and predator. Even if the temperature rises just a few degrees and the twilight shifts only by a few moments, that can mean that the timing between the flowering and the creature that takes advantage of that flowering are disrupted.

Today we see more and more plants that remain untouched by insects and never bloom. A group of Swiss researchers decided to study pollination in an area still relatively untouched at the foot of the Alps, where the flowering meadows rest in night's darkness in the shadow of the mountains. Every night, almost three hundred different insect species visit the vast meadows and the moist grasslands to pollinate about sixty varieties of flowers. One plant receiving nocturnal visits is the cabbage thistle, which attracts insects from near and far with its appealing scents, abundant pollen and nectar, and flower heads that reflect ultraviolet light. The researchers chose to study one hundred cabbage thistles spread across ten meadows. Half of these were allowed to remain in the dark, while the others were lit by lamps of a variety common in today's streetlights. When the trials were finished, it turned out that the number of visits by insects to the illuminated thistles were as much as 62 per cent lower. And in the end, they also had less fruit. The pollinators, mainly moths, simply never reached any of the flowers, and the pollination attempts were literally fruitless.

THE FIREWORKS OF THE SEA

On an August weekend in Bohuslän in the 1990s, I anchored a boat in a natural harbour in the company of two friends. One night, everything was completely still, and the late-summer darkness blurred the line between the surface of the sea and the night air, with the temperature of the water the same as the air. Diving from the boat into the water felt like throwing oneself out into space. Stuck in my memory are the fireworks of blue light that exploded the second my body cut through the surface. Every microscopic dinoflagellate in the water reacted instinctively by lighting its built-in lamp, and I dragged a trail of light behind me through the dark, salty water.

The phenomenon goes by the name of sea-fire, and we experience it in late summer and early autumn, while the sea is still lukewarm. The little lights of the dinoflagellates protect them against copepods, which are small crustaceans. The light is triggered by touch, but also by fragrance, and the glow scares off the predators. The light can also attract larger fish that eat the copepods. The dinoflagellates are, however, not the only organisms in the sea that glow. Between algae, sea squirts, crustaceans, starfish, worms, jellyfish and molluscs, there are living creatures everywhere in our oceans with the ability to produce light in one way or another, if not by themselves then in co-operation with bacteria. Just among fish, there are about 1,500 glowing species that we know of. As mentioned earlier, this phenomenon is called bioluminescence.

The dark and unknown deep ocean is a world completely different from our own, and there, darkness is the norm and light only comes for short visits. Life shows itself in flashing streaks and blinking nodes, and in between, it is completely black. To our eyes it would be perceived as a ghostly and foreign dimension not meant for us. But being able to distinguish silhouettes in the feeble daylight trickling down from the surface, or seeing other organisms' sudden fireworks, could mean the difference between life and death.

The legendary giant squid is equipped with huge eyes up to 27 centimetres in diameter, the largest in the entire animal kingdom. It took some time before scientists found out what the large eyes were good for, but it is detecting large objects, namely whales. The main adversaries of giant squids are sperm whales. Reaching 20 metres long, the wide-ranging whales can dive 2 kilometres deep in just one breath and easily devour a squid. But every movement from the whale generates tiny flashing lights from the organisms around it. The bioluminescence of small marine animals and microscopic algae can in this way function as a warning sign for the giant squids.

But even in clear water, light disperses so quickly that objects, no matter how big they are, seem to disappear when they are viewed from a distance. Humans can only see at a distance of around 33 feet, or 10 metres, even in the clearest of waters. The giant squid however, with its plate-sized eyes, is able to perceive the cloud of light caused by sperm whales at a distance of up to 120 metres. The light has by then faded out into the water and is nothing but a cold, blurry glow. The sperm whales, in return, hunt with the help of echoes from sounds within their range. Their clicking sounds are sent out through the oceans at an incredible 230 decibels, in a sound wave strong enough to break the chest bones of a human and kill them. Earthquakes are the only other phenomenon that can cause sounds that powerful. The sounds bounce off potential prey, revealing to the sperm whale what's hiding in the deep.

Ocean life is several hundred million years older than terrestrial life and still not fully explored. The organisms that existed in the ancient oceans probably also used bioluminescence to communicate and confound. But it's only in the dark abyss or in the pitch dark of night that it is possible to experience their fireworks. The dinoflagellates have a strict circadian rhythm, and after sunset, they glitter on the surface waters. With any light disruption, the effect is gone. Take a nighttime swim in the glow of the streetlights and the sea-fire effect won't happen. In order to study these organisms more closely, the scientists need to swap day for night, either their own or the dinoflagellates', and simulate a true night.

At the Scripps Institution of Oceanography in San Diego, where the California sun blazes, there is utter darkness in the inner laboratories. Only faint, red lights are used to indicate the way to the laboratory benches, where dinoflagellates crackle like sparklers in all kinds of Erlenmeyer flasks (special flasks with a flat bottom, conical body and short neck), jars and glass containers. Here, the intention is to let the dinoflagellates thrive in the safe embrace of darkness to study what happens on a chemical level when light emittances are triggered, partly out of sheer curiosity and partly because the US navy is eager to learn how to trace unknown vessels in the oceans using natural bio-light. From satellites in orbit it's possible to detect ships and submarines thanks to the light emittances of microscopic life. They are revealed by kilometre-long tracks, like chalk lines through the depths.

The light-carrying protein luciferin, which brings out the glow in sea-fire, glow-worms and fireflies, is also used in medical research as an indicator of cancer cells. Luciferin has also been used to track bacteria in fruit and veg and to look for life in space. The name of course originates from Lucifer, the bearer of light, even though the name today more likely brings about associations of the dark. The moon goddess Diana is also called Diana Lucifera thanks to her guidance during nights of the full moon. Nowadays, it is no longer necessary to collect animals with bioluminescence in order to extract the protein as it can be mass-produced by chemical means.

But we are a long way from thoroughly understanding the chemistry created by darkness in the creatures of the natural world.

WHERE THE SEA WAITS

In the BBC series *Planet Earth II*, there's a well-known scene in which sea turtle eggs hatch on a beach. In the background you can see the moon reflecting on the waves, and along the horizon there's a sliver of weak light from the sun's last rays. The tiny turtles waste no time, and as soon as they are out of their eggs, they start crawling across the beach and into the sea towards the still-light horizon in the west. They all hatch more or less at the same time, which is critical to their survival. Frigatebirds, gulls, crabs and raccoons lurk everywhere, and few turtles succeed in making it all the way down to the edge of the beach. Only one in a thousand of those who reach the sea will later survive to adulthood, and that's the way it's been for all of time.

But then the cameras pan, and behind the beach viewers can see a towering city. Streetlights, billboard, cars and lights from dwellings and shops outshine the weakly glowing horizon. The turtles, which have their origin in the Triassic Period more than 200 million years ago, have no reason to believe anything other than that the direction where the light is coming from strongest is west, where the sea waits. They trust their instinct to follow the light.

Some of the turtles closest to the edge of the beach are able to choose the right direction and swim quickly away, happily unaware of what's going on behind them. When the camera zooms out, it becomes clear that the majority of the newly hatched turtles are moving away from the sea, towards the lights of the city instead.

In that particular instance, the film team were able to save a large number of the turtles going astray, but on beaches around the world, there are too many turtles falling victim to the misleading light. One of every thousand that reach the water survive, but the problem is that ever fewer are reaching the water. On one beach in Turkey, researchers calculated that the light from nearby industries and tourist resorts meant that only two-fifths of the turtles found their way out into the waves, and in that case, the beach was still relatively dark.

Nature films are often seasoned with human melodrama, and we project our own feelings onto animal behaviours as we would with a Hollywood film. In the scene with the turtles, a single camera movement was enough to understand how tragically obliviously the young turtles wandered off in completely the wrong direction. And suddenly, we understood the seriousness of the harmful effects of light pollution on our planet. Artificial light isn't only one of mankind's most amazing inventions, it can without a doubt also be detrimental to life itself. It can displace 200 million years of instinct in an instant.

Many different species of turtle come to the beaches of Nicaragua every year, among them the ridley sea turtle, the green sea turtle, the leatherback turtle and the loggerhead turtle. All of them are on the International Union for Conservation of Nature's Red List of Threatened Species, and they are becoming ever rarer. In Nicaragua, the situation is exacerbated by the old tradition of collecting and eating sea turtle eggs. Less affluent people in particular, who have few other options, see turtle eggs as a chance for income. Now, non-profit forces have managed to raise money to hire park rangers, women only, who patrol the beaches. They buy back the eggs from collectors, spread information, pick up debris and guide the young turtles at dawn. They've succeeded well enough that nine out of ten eggs that would previously have ended up on the restaurant table today avoid that fate. But other dangers remain.

Those turtle hatchlings that do find their way into the water, despite everything, are born swimmers. Without parents and older relatives to rely on, they must navigate themselves out into the great ocean. They begin their journey at dusk and move forwards into the growing darkness. It was once thought that the hatchlings were left completely to the forces of the sea, too weak to swim towards goals they'd determined themselves, and simply drifted with the currents with chance as their only companion. Like the eel's enigmatic migrations to and from the Sargasso Sea, the turtles' spectacular migrations have been a bit of a mystery. Unlike eels, however, turtles are relatively easy to track by satellite with GPS. It's now known that the young turtles can control their fate very well by actively swimming towards nutrient-rich areas in the world's oceans. Many turtles actually seem to find their way to the same place as the eels, the Sargasso Sea, where they live under the protection of the huge patches of brown algae called sargassum. In adulthood, the turtles begin the journey home to their native beaches, and with the help of a magnetic sense, like that of birds, they can with compass-like accuracy navigate thousands of kilometres of open sea.

ROMANCE IN THE MOONLIGHT

There's a scene in the animated film *Finding Nemo* where we meet sea turtles on a trip through the sea on their way to their native beaches to lay eggs where they themselves were born. They get help from, among other things, the East Australian Current, which lets them surf along the coast of Australia, past the Great Barrier Reef in a southerly direction and then further east, north of New Zealand. The stream is 100 kilometres wide, moving at the equivalent of 16,000 swimming pools every second, and the animals are many that voluntarily or involuntarily follow along. The East Australian Current is part of the South Pacific Current, one of the five great currents that circulate water throughout the globe.

Finding Nemo is about a clownfish who's looking for his missing son, and it was awarded an Oscar for best animated film in 2003. Despite the good reviews, sales success and packed cinemas, few people suspected that the film would turn the real clownfish into a billion-dollar industry. Demand for the orange-and-white fish increased throughout the world, and the number of specimens taken from the sea multiplied. The film's message – that the fish belong in the sea – in part had the opposite effect.

But at the same time, coral reefs, with their fantastic diversity, have recently been receiving at least some of the attention they deserve, and today, the captive breeding of, for example, clownfish, is more profitable than the wild capture of them. The Saving Nemo Conservation Fund was founded in 2013 to protect clownfish and contribute to the survival of the coral reef. The foundation conducts both research and education and is based at Flinders University in Adelaide.

The clownfish is also called the anemone fish, and the reason for that is simple. Namely, the fish spends the greater part of its life among the tentacles of a sea anemone, which is something that would occur to few other animals to do. The anemone is a kind of nettle, just as corals and jellyfish are, and it fires its nettle cells at anything that comes too close. The poison burns like acid and paralyses smaller animals, which the sea anemone then eats. In fact, its poison also appears to kill cancer cells, making anemones highly interesting for medical research. The clownfish fares well against this poison thanks to a nettle-resistant mucous layer that they have. The mucus gets activated the first time a clownfish fry comes into contact with an anemone, and thereafter it can live safely within its tentacles. The species benefit from one another. The anemone protects the clownfish, and the clownfish shares its food scraps and chases off the butterfly fish, which would otherwise eat the anemones.

Nemo, the main character in *Finding Nemo*, isn't like the other clownfish. He is drawn by the steep drops into the deep sea and adventure beyond his reef, which then leads to his usually-so-cautious father having to find his way across the vast ocean to find his son. In real life, clownfish are more like Nemo's father, never taking themselves more than a few metres from the sea anemone. Sometimes, a dozen fish live in the same anemone, but never more than one sexually mature couple at a time; a great matriarch and a dominant male that is subordinate only to her. The two hold the other fish in line and do what they can to maintain their primary roles within the group. If the matriarch dies, her partner changes gender and becomes female. A younger fish can then take a seat next to her as the dominant male in the group. And when the light of the full moon breaks through the waves and finds its way through the tentacles of their home, then the couple begins their mating ritual.

The behaviour of the clownfish is controlled by natural light and darkness, and everywhere along the reefs of the world, the mating dance can be seen in the pale light of the moon. After mating, the eggs are placed in safe storage inside defensive walls of nettle cells, and they always hatch a few hours after sunset, never in daylight or even in the weak light of dusk. Darkness is crucial for the future of the clownfish.

Researchers at Flinders University and the Saving Nemo Conservation Fund have studied clownfish for several years and through experimental processes shown that just a small amount of unwanted light interferes with their mating cycle. If it's too bright, no fry are born. Not a single one. But if it gets dark, the eggs hatch, and small, transparent fry float to the surface. There they remain for a couple of weeks, growing until they are young clownfish, ready to swim down to the reef and look for their own sea anemones to settle in, eventually to become one half of a dominant couple and play in the full moonlight. Artificial light near to coral reefs disrupts this process and threatens generations of clownfish.

All along our coasts, cities spread out and the beaches attract tourists seeking experiences high on their bucket lists. Snorkelling through coral reefs among a multitude of fish above anemones, algae, starfish and crabs is a magnificent thing to be a part of.

As pleasantly vivid and colourful as the reef is to experience, the waters that surround it feel dizzying in equal measure. Where the precipices suddenly emerge and the ocean swallows the light from above, there begins eternity. As a human being, it's easy to understand the clownfish's hesitation about the deep blue of the abyss but also the allure that Nemo feels. What's really out there? As a tourist, of course, you want to get as close as possible, close to both the lively reef and the precipice over nothingness beyond that. Hotels are built directly alongside the water, with neon signs that beckon us to entertainment and spotlights that illuminate the promenades. Luxurious bungalows are placed directly on top of the coral reefs. Not infrequently, these luxury suites have glass floors to make the travel experience complete. The feeling of living on the reef, of looking out on the bustling life there and out towards the blue depths of eternity from the safety of your own sea anemone is truly enticing. It's giddying and dazzling, and we're happy to pay for that feeling.

But light leaks out through the glass floor, even if it's only faint, atmospheric lighting. From the boardwalk, spotlights sweep around, glittering off the water, and the waves reflect the facades of the ever-illuminated hotels. Dusk is protracted and never leaves room for any real night. There's no darkness. The clownfish don't know when it is time to play, the laid eggs remain unhatched at the bottom of the anemone nest, and their ancient interplay with the sea anemones slowly ends. From a human perspective, we take a step further away from the answer to the mystery of cancer when sea anemone populations decrease alongside those of the clownfish.

The Saving Nemo Conservation Fund – defender of the clownfish and coral reefs – believes that the problem is not unique to clownfish. Many reef fish behave in similar ways, having crucial periods of hatching during the night, which is why light pollution, along with warmer sea temperatures, is an important piece of the puzzle in answering why so many of the earth's coral reefs are threatened with extinction. The earth's most colourful and bustling ecosystems are slowly turning into worn-out, grey ruins.

PALE CORAL

Corals are animals called cnidarians that live completely surrounded by their protective shells, which slowly build into large reef-formations. The shell harbours not only the coral animal, but also algae, which like all plants know the art of photosynthesis. The algae give the reef its resplendent colours, enticing both wildlife and human beings to investigate its twists and turns, cavities and secret spots, searching for living things. Corals and algae have developed an intricate collaboration and are entirely dependent on one another for their well-being. It's when the algae die that the coral reef's colours fade. This phenomenon has been known for a long time as something that recurs at intervals of just over twenty years, in particular during difficult *El Niño* years.

El Niño is a regular weather phenomenon in the Pacific and Indian Oceans, which every three to five years makes the trade winds change. The warm surface water that usually follows the circulating ocean currents west along the equator instead gathers off the coast of South America. The usually cold waters are drained of fish, and rainstorms pull in over the steppe lands as the rainforest dries out.

It's under these kinds of conditions that warm water kills algae in great numbers, drains the coral reef of colour and in due course causes malnutrition in the coral. As long as the coral bleaching only takes place every twentieth year, the reef is able to recover. The quick-growing corals need about a decade to regain their previous lustre after a powerful bleaching. But the intervals between the coral bleachings have been reduced markedly; the currents aren't as stable as they were, and the temperature on earth is rising. Coral bleaching is happening as frequently as every six years, and the world's reefs are slowly being broken down. In 2017, nearly two-thirds of the Great Barrier Reef off the coast of Australia was affected by unusually warm water.

Ironically enough, it's also when the water is the warmest, in the month of December, that the corals reproduce, at least in Australia. This happens once a year and it happens, exactly as in the case of the clownfish, under the full moon. The first sign that something is starting to happen is that tiny eggs float to the surface above the reef. The eggs have been released from the interior of the coral, and within a few minutes, there will be millions of them floating around in the water. The corals are hermaphrodites, that is to say both male and female, and release their eggs and sperm at the same time. The more densely the species release their gametes – sex cells – the greater the chance of fertilisation. Individuals that start too early or get behind have less of a chance of propagating just their genes. The performance can be compared to a snow globe, which, when you turn it over for a moment, is filled with whirling snow. The whole event is a little surrealistic in tropical water at nearly 32 degrees Celsius. When the millions of sex cells reflect the full moon's light, the light from the pairings can be seen for miles out into the night's darkness.

On the way to the surface, the gametes pair up and the eggs are fertilised, giving rise to a free-swimming larva and eventually a sessile polyp. It will be another year until the next opportunity, when the adult corals once again release their gametes into the moonlit water. Many are the researchers sitting and waiting in boats above, absorbed in the experience and getting insight into the life of corals.

The synchronised snowstorm of sex cells is dictated by, among other things, the moon's predictable cycle and the rays of the sunset's final phase. The inner clock of the corals is calibrated to the latter in order to time the mating as optimally as possible. Different coral species are programmed slightly differently, but within one and the same species, they're all basically able to interact. Or they were. All around the world, reefs' alarm bells are starting to go off at the wrong time and the common mating night is being extended by several weeks. Possible explanations are the inflow of water that is too warm and the accompanying algal death, and also toxic pollution. Another reason may be that the moon is no longer as clearly visible. The corals don't know when there's a new moon or full moon because the light from the world's big cities mask the clues from the sky. The combination of global warming and light pollution doesn't simply cause coral reefs to collapse; the tiny animals also find it difficult to rebuild their structures. They need the light so that their life partners – the algae – can photosynthesise, creating energy and nutrition. But they need the darkness, too, to release their sex cells in their unison dance, thereby ensuring future larvae, polyps and reefs.

On the coral reefs, countless animals live in the kind of diversity that can only be compared with a rainforest. One of these animals is the palolo worm, a bristle worm that lives in the cavities and crevices of reef formations. Every year, when October turns to November, the worms detach the terminal parts of their bodies, which are filled with sex cells. As with corals, this happens only when the full moon is shining, and soon there are worm ends to be seen floating around the shallow waters in almost infinite number. Pacific islanders have for centuries been aware of this event on their calendars, as the palolos are an important nutritional supplement.

Many other bristle worms, such as the lugworm and ragworm, are also governed by the moon's cycle. The lugworms live in tidal zones, and we often see traces of them on our beaches in the form of their waste shaped into small, spiralled mounds of sand. We find the ragworm on harder ground or among fields of eelgrass. The colourful, 5-centimetre-long worms build small, transparent tubes in which to live. In the spring or early summer, they undergo a transformation and prepare themselves for mating. Just in time for the new moon, when the water at the surface is at its darkest, they gather in large groups to perform a swirling wedding dance, pirouetting and spiralling. The behaviour has been recreated in marine labs and aquariums, but a strict lunar cycle is required for mating to start. And the more you look, the more marine organisms you'll find that rely on signals from the lunar cycle, often in combination with other clues such as sunlight levels or water temperature. Species of sea pens, fish, crabs and molluscs depend on the moon's recurring changes to know when the next phase of life is to begin.

THE TWILIGHT ZONE

I floated with my arms outstretched. The midday sun splintered in the waves, giving the ancient limestone formations every conceivable colour. Below me mingled fish, starfish, snails and bristle worms; algae swayed slowly back and forth. I was travelling through Honduras visiting a small part of the world's second largest reef, the Mesoamerican Barrier Reef System. It was only a few metres deep above the corals, but as soon as I drew near to the edge, I saw the deep sea come towards me. Every glance out past the reef made me vertiginous, as if I were looking over the world's end, the very edge of eternity. The light turquoise of the water quickly changed to deep blue, and all the contours grew blurry just tens of metres away. Sometimes I could make out shadows, as if shoals of big fish were approaching, or as if darkness itself was forming into life. I was reminded of scenes from *The Big Blue*, Luc Besson's film about the free diver Jacques Mayol. He was the first to dive to a depth of 100 metres without breathing equipment. I saw before me how his headtorch grew all the more desolate the further down he went, and the way his calm leg strokes took him deeper and deeper downwards, unconcerned with the eternity that grew around him. I'm not particularly afraid of heights, nor of the dark, but this made me light-headed and nearly panic-stricken. Even so it was incredibly fascinating to gaze down at the abyss.

The light from the surface decreases rapidly in the sea; 200 metres deep, there isn't much of it remaining. But it's still possible to measure a faint, single-hued turquoise sliver of light as far down as a kilometre. We would experience it as pitch darkness, but the zone extending down to 1,000 metres is nonetheless called the twilight zone of the sea. The eternal night first begins below it. At those depths, the only light to be seen comes from the organisms that create it themselves with the help of bioluminescence. The eyes that peer out into the endless darkness respond to the slightest glimmer of light, ten times weaker than what we ourselves are able to pick up. What we consider to be total darkness actually has many nuances.

Twice a day, the earth's largest migration takes place. Plankton, crustaceans, molluscs, small fish and a wide range of other organisms move between the dark volumes of water in the ocean depths and the lighter water at the surface. Not only in the seas, but also in the lakes. Every night, millions of animals rise to the surface and then slowly sink again when dawn arrives. All these organisms have consistent internal clocks, governed by the earth's rotation and the changes in light throughout the course of the day. Their inner rhythm moves at a predetermined pace, but the timing is calibrated by the light, so the movement matches up with the hours in the day.

At the poles, where the contrast between summer and winter is greatest, this rhythm pauses during the midnight sun. And in the winter, when it's constantly night, the moon takes over as director and regulates the timings with its orbit. The monthly reappearance of the bright full moon also affects the oceans – wherever on earth it appears, migration is temporarily halted. Contrastingly, a solar eclipse sets the sea in motion in the middle of the day.

Changes in natural light affect entire ecosystems, the reason being that darkness is synonymous with security. As daylight penetrates further and further into the depths, the animals stay in the protective black waters, because the darkness serves as a protection, a way for the small, often microscopic, organisms to avoid being eaten by predatory fish. Typically, they're at their most vulnerable when the moon temporarily appears, or early at dawn when they are suddenly clearly visible in the first rays of the morning sun.

We see the need for the protection of darkness further up the food chain, too. Eels only migrate when the moon is shaded and the lights are out. Illuminated waterways make the fabled fish hide in the sediment on the bottom and wait it out for the seemingly eternal day. In the River Säveån, near Gothenburg, Sweden, where eels have been counted and their movements mapped, it's been noted that considerably more pass by when the moon is below the horizon than when its light is shining. During one of the eel-counting nights, late in September in 2012, a power outage occurred at a nineteenth-century factory. The whole area around the red brick buildings built in the 1830s fell into darkness. The night became longer and its darkness deeper; the song of the particoloured bats could be heard along the southern banks of the Säveån. On this night, the activity of the eels was particularly pronounced.

Other fish react to light, too. Perch, for example, sense very small light changes, and an amount of light equivalent to one-tenth of the full moon affects their circadian rhythm. Maybe the fact that the typical amount of light in the lake and sea is so small makes the fish extra sensitive. It's also been observed that migrating salmon are most frequently caught by seals when the waters suddenly light up, naturally or – as is becoming more common – unnaturally. Illuminated estuaries and harbour basins can work to the benefit of predators such as seals, at least temporarily. We have really known this for a long time. As mentioned earlier, fishermen have used lanterns for centuries to attract fish . In northern Norway, where trawlers hunt herring and the seine nets enclose tonnes of fish every day, humans aren't the only ones taking advantage of the catch. Killer whales hear the sounds of fishing boats in the distance, and when they reach the light from the ship, they're able to hunt without the use of sonar. By signalling with bubbles, like smoke signals, illuminated by the artificial light, the killer whales attract their relatives so that they can also take part in the buffet. The break in northern darkness gives killer whales an advantage as light changes the rules of the game and the balance between predator and prey. But it's only now that we're starting to think about the consequences of this.

In the sea off Wales, oil rigs and large ships are giving off light to an increasing extent. Despite the knowledge that artificial light can affect various organisms, marine animals are still relatively unstudied in this context. So two British universities launched a study on light pollution in 2013. Plastic panels equipped with LEDs were lowered a little below the surface of the Menai Strait between the island of Anglesey and the British mainland. Then the growth of various organisms was measured over time. Forty-seven different groups of organisms settled on the panels in intricate miniature ecosystems. Immobile animals such as corals and tubular bristle worms formed small landscapes, inhabited by crustaceans, larvae and fish fry. But the more illuminated the panels were, the lower the diversity, benefiting only a few species of animal. It was especially clear that sea urchins and cnidarians chose dark panels while collembola and bristle worms thrived as well or better on the illuminated panels, despite the fact that the mating rituals of the bristle worms are governed by the variations of moonlight. With light equivalent to that of normal street lighting, the researchers were able to control the design of the small ecosystems.

On a larger scale this dynamic is, of course, concerning. There are about a hundred thousand merchant and transport ships sailing between the earth's continents, and there are 1,500 oil rigs and at least a hundred larger wind farms out in the sea. Forty per cent of the world's population lives within 100 kilometres of a coastal area, and the pressure on our seas is constantly increasing. For the moment, much of the great oceans may still lie under a pristine night sky, but you have to get further and further out from land if the starlight is going to appear in all its full splendour and the creatures of the sea are to live undisturbed by man-made light.

ECOSYSTEM IN FLUX

There are a lot of strange creatures living on New Zealand. The islands' distant location far from other land masses has allowed evolution to roar on freely for 125 million years, ever since the islands disconnected from Antarctica, Africa and South America in the common landmass called Gondwanaland. The only two native mammals are bat species, which sometimes give their wings a rest and instead run around the ground eating both pollen and insects. In the absence of predators, several bird species have stopped flying and been found to settle into their own niches on the ground. A number of insects have also developed a behaviour that we are not used to seeing in similar species in other parts of the world. One of the more spectacular of these is the weta. Wetas actually encompass several different species and genera of grasshoppers. They look like bush crickets (*Tettigoniidae*) with slightly more prickly legs, but they lack wings and rarely jump around. Instead, they crawl on the ground, ideally at night. The spectacular thing about wetas is that they can grow large and above all heavy. Specimens of 10 centimetres are not uncommon, and the record weight is put at 70 grams. That was admittedly a female with eggs, but no less impressive for that. The weight matches that of a sparrow or five New Zealand bats. In Sweden, we'd need to put an extra stamp on a letter of that weight in order to send it by post.

The weta's nocturnal habits reflect the fact that earlier in time there were large birds that would more than happily eat insects of the weta's calibre. With few exceptions, the birds were diurnal, which is why wetas preferred the darkness of night to gather food. They still had enemies, including one in the form of the nocturnal tuatara, a reptile unique to New Zealand, which is not closely related to either contemporary lizards or crocodiles and has been sitting all alone on its branch of the family tree for at least 225 million years. But the ground was still by far the safest place for wetas at night, at least until today.

In the 1800s, when Europeans started coming in ever-larger groups with their pets, the number of predators increased markedly. Cats, in particular, have been hard on the New Zealand fauna since their arrival. Few of the wild animals had the necessary defences to deal with new foes, and many native species, including the large grasshoppers, have found it increasingly difficult. Their worst enemies today are the rats, which seafarers – albeit highly involuntarily – brought to New Zealand as early as the 1700s. Rats, like so many other mammals, prefer to be out at dusk, which is why it has been suggested that we should be able to protect the domestic wildlife with the help of artificial light. Possibly both rats and cats would kill fewer New Zealand animals if it was a little brighter. The idea may sound reasonable were it not for the fact that the prey animals would also be affected. Night and day have followed each other in exactly the same way in the southern hemisphere as in the north throughout the millions of years. Animals' rhythms have adjusted to that, and New Zealand is obviously no exception. It's also been demonstrated that the weta reacts very strongly to light, never leaving its hole until the sun has set below the horizon. On nights when there's a full moon, the animal stays at home. In one experiment, it was shown that most wetas – nearly 90 per cent – completely eschew looking for food in artificially lit environments. And it doesn't help that rats also avoid the light.

On islands where new predators appear, either naturally or having been brought there by humans, the prey animals usually end up at a disadvantage quickly. They lack the defences required as they've never before had to protect themselves against these kinds of predators, neither during their own lifetimes nor in the history of their ancestors. A long process of natural selection of behaviours and characteristics is required for predators and prey to reach a balance, which humans and their pets easily overturn.

Another effective way to upset ecosystems and the balance between predator and prey is altering the environment. When we illuminate our evenings and nights, we not only confuse animals' circadian rhythms so that they no longer know when they should be hiding or when they should be out hunting; we also eliminate the possibility of camouflage and reveal the hiding places of both prey and predator. A tiger that hunts at dusk relies on its stripes blending in with the grass until it becomes an invisible figure in the shadows, but in the increasing skyglow from the great cities of Asia, the tiger is becoming easier to detect. It's rare that such changes impact both sides equally.

Some species can be winners – such as rats. Other species cannot find food. In the case of the increased numbers of streetlamps, in which opportunistic bats catch moths, there are two losers. The moths, which can avoid most chasing bats in the dark, have completely lost their defence when they're in the glow of the streetlamp. But even those bat species that typically can actually outsmart moths – the barbastelle and brown-long-eared – are losing out through this change. These butterfly-eaters belong to the most light-averse of the bats and don't have access to the buffet table under the lights but instead are pushed further and further away into the peripheral landscape.

THE THREAT TO THE BATS

In 1875, Jenny Alfrida Jonsson was born; she later married Johan Eklöf and was the mother of my future maternal grandfather. Just as on my grandfather's father's side, Jenny's family and their relatives had their roots in the Tidaholm area from a very long time ago. She was baptised in Suntak's church, which was built as early as the 1130s in the midst of old Iron Age graves. The church was outfitted with an apse, a crescent-shaped extension for the chancel, which showed that the community could boast of a good economy. Queen Kristina's page and cavalry master, Erik Hård af Segerstad (1621–92), lies buried under the church's rough wooden floor, and his coat of arms adorns the wall. Although the church has been expanded in stages, it has nevertheless been able to preserve its Romanesque character to this day, perhaps thanks to the fact that a new church was built a few hundred metres away during the nineteenth century.

Someone visiting at dusk will find the bats chasing each other around Suntak's church, surrounded by the limestone and sandstone walls. A colony of brown long-eared bats has found refuge from the wind and is in place to birth a new litter. Each female has only one offspring per year, and the entire colony helps to take care of its collective progeny. The brown long-ears are, like most bats, homebodies that usually return to the same place every year – and often for decades. Bats can grow to be older than you'd think. The oldest bat we're aware of is a forty-one-year-old from the Russian taiga. Considering the power of habit, perhaps the long-eared bats and their ancestors have been inhabiting the church in Suntak ever since my great-grandmother's baptism, perhaps even since it was built in the twelfth century, marking the span of multiple historical ages.

In Västgötaslätten, there are a lot of old churches: there are more per square kilometre than anywhere else in Sweden, with the sole exception of Gotland. The buildings and their immediate surroundings have been tended in the same way throughout the centuries and have therefore become important oases, not just for people seeking calm but also for animals and plants. Actually, our churches and cemeteries have changed very little over time, and many animals that have lived close to them have largely been left in peace. As recently as the 1980s, bats were considered pests. Few people had really bothered to look at them, let alone study them. But Jens Rydell at Lund University took an inventory of bat colonies at a number of churches in Sjuhärad and Skaraborg. It turned out that about two-thirds of the churches were inhabited by distinct bat colonies that hunted around the towers, ate flies in the attics and took care of their new offspring every summer. The females often stayed in the attics while a lone male moved into the tower, at a proper distance.

Just over thirty years after the inventory of Västergötland's church attics, the church environments were no longer untouched. In the 1990s, a trend in lighting started that has today escalated to become almost a competition between the districts. Increasingly strong lights are pointed at the steeples, naves and apses. The graves swim in spotlights, and the pathways towards the churchyards are bedecked with lanterns. Bat refuge in the dark attics is threatened. The darkness has been expelled.

We retrieved data in the 1980s; now it was just a matter of redoing the same set. For two years, we searched nearly a hundred churches in Västergötland. We climbed towers, crawled around in attics and listened in the cemeteries. In the best cases, we could see clusters of bats under the roofs, at rest or grooming their fur, barking or taking care of their pups. We found bats hiding in the innermost part of a church while renovations were under way, sitting there despite thunder and the chimes of the church bells, and we found bats as they came out one by one through small openings under the eaves and disappeared under the protection of the nearest tree. Soon it was possible for us to predict exactly where they would fly out. With few exceptions, they chose the darkest and shadiest tree or shrub with the shortest flight distance from the rooftop. But no longer did two-thirds of the churches have their own bat colonies, it was only a third. In churches where darkness still reigns, such as Suntak's old church, they still live. In churches that have their facades lit up, they're gone, which has prompted their entry on the Swedish Red List, that is the list of endangered species.

When we looked at the results a little more closely, we could see that there were some bats remaining in some of the illuminated churches, but only in those where the facade lights were turned off before midnight. So, it's possible to keep the bats for as long as you let the night prevail at least to some degree through fairly simple means. Then we can, of course, consider whether we really need to light up our church environments as though they were amusement parks. But really that's an unjust comparison. Liseberg (an amusement park in Gothenburg, Sweden's second largest city) on an August evening is actually less illuminated than the car park next to it.

As long as the churches are outfitted with spotlights, the bats don't dare emerge. In their eyes, the day is still going in full swing and dangers await in the light. Females with newborn pups need to get a lot of food, but the false daylight prevents them doing so. In England, bats in these kinds of situations starve to death rather than choose to move away from their homes. At the same time, the smorgasbord is set out right there. The spotlights attract caddisflies, moths, swarming beetles and flies. The gathering of insects is sometimes exploited by the fastest and most opportunistic bat species, which dive into the beams of light, snatching some prey for themselves and quickly escaping into the darkness again. The brown long-ears inside the church attic can only sit by and observe, waiting for darkness.

The diminishing numbers of brown long-ears was the first sign that things were worsening for many bats in Sweden, a trend that has long been supported by anecdotal narratives. When I'm out in the countryside talking with the residents during my nature inventories, I often hear that the number of bats has decreased. They talk about how the nocturnal animals used to sweep around the corners of the houses at twilight, catching mosquitoes by the front steps. But that today they're rarely to be seen. I'm gifted now and then with stories and anecdotes about how the children in the villages threw caps in the air to catch flying bats or about how the bat silhouettes used to follow fly fishermen at the streams or investigate the drying white laundry on the lines in the garden. That bats can be attracted by white sheets seems to be widely circulated lore, but I've never found any real evidence for it.

Today, we know that things are also going badly for northern bats, which have always been considered one of our most common species of bat. Within thirty years, they've decreased by as much as 60 per cent. In April of 2020, both northern bats and the brown long-ears were included on the Swedish Red List.

NIGHT SERVICES

Bats were blamed for the Covid-19 virus outbreak and painted, as so many times before, as creatures of terror. But despite similarities to a virus found in the horseshoe bat branch of the bat order, it's not clear where the SARS-CoV-2 virus actually came from. Normally, bats rarely infect people with viruses, although of course it can occur. Better we should learn from bats' unique immune systems, which have been trained to manage diseases over millions of years.

Anyone who's ever sworn at mosquitoes should welcome bats. A single bat can eat three thousand insects in one night, and a colony can make a big difference in the comfort felt on a terrace on quiet summer evenings. It may well be that bats are working towards their own ends, but we gratefully enjoy their work. In Asia, rice is the most important food for billions of people, but crops are constantly threatened by attacks from insects and diseases.

Every year, more than 100 million tonnes of rice are disposed of because for various reasons they can't be eaten. Above the wet fields, bats do their best to reduce those losses, eating tonnes of insects that would otherwise have gone after the rice. Few pesticides are as effective, and few are equally organic and natural. In Thailand alone, bats' services are estimated to be worth 100 million dollars every year. Something similar applies in North

America. Every night, more than 100 million bats take off from caves and bridges in the southern states of the United States, and each individual can eat more than half its bodyweight in one day. That means 500 tonnes of insects in a single night. Among their prey we find owlet moths, whose larvae do great damage to maize and cotton crops. The bats' appetite saves approximately three billion dollars for US growers every year, money that otherwise would have to be spent on pesticides.

Just like hummingbirds, bumblebees, honeybees and moths, many bats seek out the flowers and fruits of plants, which makes them important pollinators. More than five hundred plants around the world rely on bats for pollination. Many of them are both common and economically important, such as agave, balsa wood, mango, guava and date. Other plants rely on bats to spread their seeds in their droppings over the tropics. In Thailand and Malaysia, the value of bat pollination to durian, or 'stinkfruit', is calculated to be about 100 million dollars annually. The durian, which can weigh up to 3 kilograms, is considered a real delicacy, which is why it's also called the king of fruits despite its strange, musty scent that often sees it banned in hotels and on public transport. However, its odour has evolved not for our sensibilities but for those of the animals that spread its seeds, such as orangutans.

Out of the world's more than 1,300 bat species, about 70 per cent are insectivores. As far back as the beginning of the twentieth century, it was realised that bats can keep large insect populations in check, including those that spread disease, such as malaria-carrying mosquitoes. Malaria today is one of mankind's absolute worst scourges, causing over 1,500 deaths daily, and there have been occasional experiments attempting to attract hungry bats to affected areas. The idea is more relevant than ever, since drug-resistant malaria has started to spread around the world. No one has yet done any comprehensive calculations of the value of maintaining bat populations in light of this, or of what would happen if the bat disappeared completely from artificially lit church towers, tourist caves and city centres. However, other, more commercial, actors have, in recent years, had their eyes opened to what bats eat and what comes out the other end.

Bat droppings, known as guano, have always been considered an effective fertiliser. In many places, it's commercially mined, and even in Sweden, you can find cans of guano at well-stocked garden centres. In our age of chemistry, however, we tend to forget such natural sources of phosphorus and other nutrients. But in 2014, when a couple, Melanie Drese and Michael Völker, took over an old vineyard in Germany, they set out to cultivate as organically and naturally as they could. So they did everything to attract bats, with darkness, water, insect-rich lands and suitable habitats. A large colony of grey long-eared bats lives in the vineyard now, producing a great quantity of free manure. The farm's most popular wine is also named Fledermaus, with a picture of a grey long-ear on the label. Their red Fledermaus from 2017 is described as an acidic, minerally wine, with hints of strawberry, lime and blackcurrants, and the grapes have grown large from the nutrients in the bat droppings.

French winegrowers have come to understand the benefits of having bats on the farm, too. The Bordeaux wine committee commissioned a study in the southwest of France, in a wine region with mediaeval origins south of Bordeaux. Over a period of three years, researchers collaborated with about twenty vineyards to get bats to establish themselves in the district. Analyses were done of what the bats ate and whether they hunted near their settlements. Predictably, nearly all the colonies that had established themselves hunted over their vines. It turned out that they also caught and ate large quantities of leafroller moths, whose larvae do great damage to the vines. In the long run, the hope is that the results will lead to the amount of pesticides being drastically reduced in France and throughout Europe.

Initiatives like these, in quantifying how much animals and plants can be worth to humans, make biologists suddenly have to talk to economists in financial terms. We have started talking about ecosystem services – the voluntary work carried out around the clock by the planet's various organisms. To a large extent, this happens at night: pollination, pest control, decomposition, carbon dioxide storage, noise reduction, medicinal chemical production – the list could go on. The more unquantifiable worth, in the form of aesthetics, the scents of flowers at dusk, birdsong and the beneficial aspects of a salt bath, are harder to translate in economic terms, but there are many studies that establish how proximity to nature helps improve our sense of well-being.

PART III:
HUMANITY AND THE COSMIC LIGHT

THREE TWILIGHTS

Light hesitates, it's not instantaneous, posited Danish astronomer Ole Rømer (1644–1710) having studied Io, one of Jupiter's moons, in 1675. Rømer was one of the first people to consider that light could have a speed. His observations became an important piece of the puzzle in our understanding of what light is. Not long after Rømer's observations, the Dutch astronomer Christiaan Huygens (1629–95) put forward the idea that light is a wave, while his contemporary Isaac Newton (1643–1727) claimed that light consisted of particles. It would turn out that they were both right.

The person who usually gets the credit for having put Huygens' and Newton's models together is Albert Einstein (1879–1955), even if he was himself a little dubious about the result. Einstein calculated that light consists of particles, *photons*, but also that it's a forward-moving wave. That is, the light has two aspects, a dual nature in which on the one hand it's something physical, with a mass, and on the other hand it's a moving field of energy. Every time the light collides with something, it's either absorbed or reflected. When it reflects and hits our eyes, we perceive the object in question.

Not until as late as 2015 could light be imaged in its two states, thereby confirming Einstein's calculations. But what we refer to as light in everyday speech is really just a small part of something larger – electromagnetic radiation. At one end of the electromagnetic spectrum are long radio waves and microwaves, and at the other end are the short waves of X-rays and gamma radiation. The light with all its colours we find in the middle, but there are thus significantly more wavelengths than we see day to day. The size of the electromagnetic wave, the wavelength, determines whether we are able to perceive it or not. Our eyes are sensitive to light wavelengths between 380 and 800 nanometres long. The wavelengths in the upper part of that range we see as red light, in the lower as violet, and in between as the rest of the colour spectrum.

Many animals can perceive wavelengths that we cannot and therefore different nuances in the environment. The light that has long wavelengths beyond our perceptual capacity we call infrared, and we feel it as heat. Snakes can combine infrared vision with other sensory impressions to create an image of their surroundings and find warm-bodied prey more easily. The light with wavelengths shorter than we can perceive we call ultraviolet, and it is used by insects and birds in a colour world beyond our own.

The way colours appear shifts throughout the course of the day. When the sun is low, its light strikes the atmosphere at an angle and so has to pass through more air molecules to reach the earth. Its short-wave, blue light is refracted more than usual and scattered even further across the sky. Meanwhile, the long-wave, red light penetrates more easily, and more of it reaches an observer on the earth's surface. As a result, the sky near the sun appears red to us, and further away it appears bluer. We experience a cycle of light that is dominated alternately by blue and red depending on whether it's morning, noon or evening. At the same time, the intensity of the light varies considerably. A sun at its zenith gives off light that is a billion times stronger than we can experience during a cloudy night with a new moon.

As daylight decreases, shadows become longer and colours

paler. We say that darkness falls, until it has set over the landscape like a heavy blanket. The constitution of the Swedish Civil Aviation Administration states: 'Darkness is the state that prevails between sunset and sunrise, when due to reduced daylight a prominent unlit object cannot clearly be distinguished at distances greater than 8 km.'

The darkness of night is contingent upon how many degrees below the horizon the sun is. But before the night with its thicker darkness comes down, the evening undergoes its metamorphosis through the three phases of twilight. A new kind of twilight occurs every 6 degrees. As the upper part of the solar disc sinks to the west, the first of the three phases begins – the civil twilight. On a cloudless night, you can still read a book in the available light then, as the very strongest stars begin to appear as hardly discernible points in the firmament: Vega, Capella and Arcturus. The North Star, which we often think of when we're talking about stars that are easy to see with the naked eye, is really quite far down the list of the brightest celestial bodies, but it can be seen steadily and reliably in the north, which is why it has become an important benchmark and a prominent symbol.

How long the twilight lasts, of course, depends on where you're located. The further north, the flatter the solar orbit is. During the spring and autumn equinoxes, civil twilight lasts about three-quarters of an hour in southern Sweden, and during the summer approximately an hour. North of the Dal River, it starts after midnight during summer and blends with the dawn, so it never really gets dark. Or as the iconic Swedish writer Harry Martinson wrote: 'The June night never happens.' And likewise, the polar nights of winter seem endless when the sun never reaches high enough to summon the day. At the equator, on the other hand, dusk falls furiously fast, regardless of the season, and each phase takes just fifteen minutes.

When the centre of the sun reaches 6 degrees below the horizon, civil twilight turns into nautical twilight. The brightest stars and the horizon are clear, which is a prerequisite for being able to navigate with the help of sextant, hence the term. The sextant was invented in 1757 by the British naval officer John Campbell (1720–90) and has had a huge impact on seafaring ever since. The idea is simple. By measuring the angle between different stars and the dimly lit horizon at specific times you can determine your geographical position. Even today, in the electronic age, the method is an important back-up out on the world's oceans.

Nautical twilight also lasts for the period of time it takes for the sun to drop 6 degrees. So, when the sun lies 12 degrees below the horizon, the last of the three twilight phases begins – the astronomical. Weaker stars are now becoming clearer, though it's not yet completely dark, and the direction of the sun is identifiable. Halfway through astronomical twilight, when the centre of the sun reaches 15 degrees below the horizon, is sometimes referred to informally as *amateur astronomical twilight*. It's called that because most of the stars and heavenly phenomena that are visible without the use of sophisticated equipment can now be seen. In writings about the Skåne-born scientist and later court astronomer in Prague Tycho Brahe (1546–1601), one reads that he was the foremost in his discipline with the naked eye; that is, completely without optical aids. His working days began halfway into nautical twilight and lasted until what is known as the hour of the wolf, deep in the night.

Recently, the Tycho Brahe Museum opened in All Saints Church on Ven, the island where Brahe spent much of his life in the service of astronomy. Anyone who visits the museum can learn more about how the Renaissance man questioned the thousand-year-old theories of the laws that were said to govern the universe and how he named no fewer than 777 stars in the firmament, after seeing them only with his naked eye. Parts of his observatory, Stjerneborg, have been restored today, but the night sky isn't the same now as at the end of the sixteenth century. The shimmer from all the city lights of the Öresund Region clouds the eyes of those who today want to use their unaided eyes in search of stars. The light pollution in the sky rubs out galaxies and distant solar systems, as if we had used a dirty cloth to wipe the window facing the universe.

DARK MATTER

Galaxies rotate too fast. They behave as if they consisted of something more, unknown to us. The question of what affects the rotation of galaxies has puzzled astronomers since the phenomenon was discovered in the early 1980s.

James Peebles came to Princeton University in 1958, only a few years after the death of Albert Einstein, and has since that time tried to solve some of the great mysteries of the universe. During his sixty years at the university, Peebles has – following in the footsteps of his famous predecessor – studied the structure and history of the universe, from the big bang's dense, hot constitution to the protracted, increasingly cold condition that now reigns. Peebles, who today lives very near Einstein's old house, has come to shape our everyday conception of the universe and greatly contributed to a larger understanding of the incomprehensible world we have around us.

Peebles's image of the universe can be likened to a dark scene where an ensemble is playing music. The few musicians we can see represent visible matter. We hear more somewhere out there in the dark, but we don't see them. We are becoming more confident that there are more musicians out there, and we can even come up with a theoretical model of how many there are and which instruments they're playing. There are a lot of them. To create what we're actually hearing requires twenty times more musicians than those we're seeing. In real terms, there is twenty times more of something unknown out there in the universe than what we can perceive with today's methods of measuring. Some of that other stuff, that which we can't see, has come to be called dark matter – completely invisible particles. They don't emit or reflect electromagnetic radiation, which is required for our eye or measuring instruments to register them. Instead, we have to rely on the effect that dark matter has on other particles through its gravitational force or, to continue the orchestral analogy, the harmony that arises from the tones between observed and unobserved musicians in the imaginary orchestra.

James Peebles' point of departure was describing something called cosmic background radiation, which has been present from the infancy of the universe, partly to confirm the big bang theory, and partly to come to the conclusion not only that dark matter exists but that there is a lot of it. Only 5 per cent of the universe consists of matter that we can see, and just over 20 per cent is made up of the enigmatic dark matter. The rest is explained, according to today's models, by the even more secretive *dark energy*, which is a key to understanding the origin of the universe. But that's outside my realm of understanding and the parameters of this book.

Today, space telescopes can image the cosmic background radiation studied by Peebles, revealing a structure, a pattern of varying radiation. And in Peebles' modern creation story, this is the design of the universe. The pattern shows how the first particles, with the help of dark matter, clumped together to become all the galaxies of the universe. He received a Nobel Prize in 2019 for this breakthrough work.

We experience vision as immediate; what we see is happening now. On earth, the distances are short enough. But light travels, too, and it takes time to arrive. The speed of light is limited; we see the sun as it looked eight minutes ago and the North Star as it appeared in the seventeenth century. In fact, we cannot be quite sure that something is even still there when we see it. The further away we're looking, the further back in time we're seeing.

If we follow the trail of microwaves – that is, the background radiation of the universe – further and further out into space – and accordingly further and further back in time – as if it were a dwindling light in the deep sea, we'll eventually encounter an impenetrable wall. All background radiation originates from here. We've reached as close to the origin of the universe as we can get, some 100 thousand years after the big bang; a wall of hot plasma soup with unsorted, free particles forming a luminous fog. Here the microwaves stop guiding us in our journey through time. But Peebles' universe goes further back than that, past the plasma soup, past the big bang, and extrapolates a creation from the unknown, before atoms and photons were created – from the moment or the entire eternity in the dark before time began, before God stepped in with his every light. Religious stories of our origins being dark and chaotic may therefore have a grain of astronomical truth in them. It may be, in fact, that the period we're living in now is just a parenthesis to the eternal life of the universe. Is this age of light and matter perhaps only a fluctuation or temporary effect of the expanding spacetime? We are born in the dark, we die in the dark. The light is just a moment and yet all life depends on it.

MEASURE OF THE NIGHT SKY

In 1744, the new year's night was lit up by one of the brightest comets in history, C/1743 X1 or the Klinkenberg-Chéseaux comet, as it's also known. This could be seen in the sky for a few months around the turn of the year 1744, at the same time as France began its quickly abandoned attempt to invade England. The future astronomer Charles Messier (1730–1817) was then just a teenager, and it was the Klinkenberg-Chéseaux comet that ignited his interest. He was to spend his life as a comet hunter, or 'comet ferret' as the French king Louis XV called him. But in practice, Messier's work was largely about locating more than just comets in the sky. He thought it would be easier to identify comets if he first sorted everything else around them, a bit like picking out all the green Lego pieces and then in peace and quiet being able to find the blue pieces.

The first object that Charles Messier picked out as a non-comet was the Crab Nebula, now known as the Messier object 1, or M1 for short. The Crab Nebula is an exploded star – a supernova remnant – first observed in 1054, which has today grown into a more than six-light-year-wide cloud of gas. Before Messier died at the age of eighty-six, he'd created a list of 103 objects that were not comets but could possibly be mistaken as such. The list of Messier objects was later expanded and now consists of 110 objects, which are widely used by astronomers in a variety of contexts. The Messier objects are, among other things, excellent for determining the quality of the night sky, that is the degree of darkness in a given place. The American amateur astronomer John E. Bortle made use of this in the early 2000s to establish a scale for night darkness – the Bortle scale. The purpose was to be able to assess how much a night sky is affected by light pollution. The scale has nine stages, where a one corresponds to a natural, completely untouched sky and a nine the grey-orange, starless sky we see above our metropolitan centres. The scale is based on how well different objects and phenomena can be observed in the sky, not least Messier objects, but also the faint ghost of zodiacal light and the Milky Way.

In the very best of night skies, rated as a stage one or two on the Bortle scale, up to six thousand stars or other objects can be seen with the naked eye, including the Triangulum Galaxy, or Messier object 33 (M33), if you'd prefer. The Triangulum Galaxy is the most distant thing that can be seen without binoculars, and in a really dark sky it can be seen as part of the Triangulum constellation. It may be one of the Milky Way's nearest neighbours, but it's still three million light-years away. This means that the light we see today from the Triangulum Galaxy started its journey at the same time as the birth of our own genus, *Homo*.

In a starry sky classified as a four on the Bortle scale, one can still, with a trained eye, locate the M33 among about two thousand other objects, but when you reach stage six, this is completely impossible. Then the number of visible stars in the sky has decreased to five hundred or fewer. It's right there, between four and six on the scale, that the artificial light from our urbanised landscapes makes itself really felt, in rural and suburban skies. This is where the Milky Way's celestial bodies – to us, pinpoints – begin fading more and more to disappear from the sky completely by stage seven. By the time we reach the top of the scale, only five to ten of the brightest objects in the sky are identifiable, and the light is a thousand times stronger than it was in an unimpacted sky.

In February of 1701, when Sweden organised a victory party in honour of the Battle of Narva the year before, they literally didn't spare the gunpowder. One hundred and thirty cannons, positioned strategically around Stockholm, fired the salute at the same time as the hymn *Te Deum Laudamus* echoed in the Great Church. When darkness fell, light arrangements were lit to pay homage to the king and the Caroleans. One of these installations was erected in Brunkeberg Square. It was a 25-metre-high wooden pyramid draped in linen, designed by the court architect himself, Nicodemus Tessin the Younger. Metre-high letters praised King Charles XII, and everything was illuminated from behind by more than two thousand whale oil lamps. In a world without cinema, television or neon signs, such displays were magnificent spectacles and displays of power. Further light displays were placed around Stockholm, with tributes to and images of the king. And in the area of the city known as Riddarholm an amphitheatre was erected, lit by a thousand lanterns. The king's light installations were a demonstration of power, and lighting is used in a similar way this very day. The Luxor Sky Beam in Las Vegas, the giant spotlight, is a clear example of that.

Author Paul Bogard begins an interesting trip through the Bortle scale in Las Vegas. In *The End of Night: Searching for Natural Darkness in an Age of Artificial Light*, Bogard goes in search of natural darkness, beginning with the unofficial capital of neon lights. In Las Vegas, the Pleiades are the only Messier object that can be discerned, and the artificial light outshines most celestial objects other than the moon and the nearest planets, Venus and

Mars. With the help of astronomers, researchers and other friends of darkness, Bogard moves on from Vegas and ever further from the light of cities, in his search for darker night skies and more magnificent cosmic experiences. Ultimately, he ends up in the Eureka Valley, which is part of Death Valley National Park. Funnily enough, the place is situated only 350 kilometres from the Las Vegas Strip, but it is still one of the darkest places on the North American continent. For Death Valley is not simply the hottest and driest region in the United States, and as such sparsely populated; it's also the lowest, with several valleys below sea level, and mountains as tall as 3,000 metres all around. So, despite its relative proximity to Las Vegas and the major Californian cities, the light is effectively blocked from disturbing the darkness of the desert night. Bogard writes that the light of the Milky Way is so intense here that it creates shadows on the ground, and the distant light from Jupiter is more than enough to disturb his night vision. The concepts of light and darkness are redefined when the darkest sky, remote from civilisation, is dazzling with its zodiacal lights and astral fireworks, while the brightest of city skies creates dark nooks and disreputable alleyways. Our perception of what's actually light and dark sometimes jibes poorly with reality.

SAINT LAWRENCE'S TEARS

Every year, when the Nordic light once again begins to give way to darker nights, the earth crosses the orbit of the Swift-Tuttle comet. The comet itself appears only once every 133 years, but in its trail along its path around the sun, a cloud of particles and dust follow. These are as small as grains of sand or as large as boulders and have been torn loose from the surface of the comet. When the earth crosses the comet's orbit, we see the particles as swarms of meteors, or shooting stars. At a speed of more than 200,000 kilometres per hour they hit the atmosphere, where they are heated by the friction with the air and become visible as thin, white, glowing streaks in the night sky. On a clear, dark night in the middle of August, thousands of these hastily drawn little lines in the sky can be seen, soon to disappear again.

A few summers ago, I wanted to try to experience the shooting stars in as undisturbed a way as possible. My family and I scrubbed our little rowboat as clean as we could and bedded it down with blankets, duvets and pillows. At midnight, we rowed out on Lake Tolken in Västergötland, where we have our summer cottage. The cottage is an inheritance from my paternal grandfather, who had it built in the 1950s, in line with the health and wellness ideals of the time. A sparsely decorated fishing cottage was good for both mind and body, Grandpa contended, and he was probably right about that. The lake view, the dark evenings and the lapping of the water do make it easy to unwind. His armchair is still there, as are his coffee cups, the painting my dad did of the old boat and the notebooks with shallows, depths and the best fishing spots written in them. Next to the sofa is the gramophone with a hand crank, and over the wood stove there still hang dried *hålkakor* (round loaves of bread) that Grandma once baked.

A bit out on the water we stayed the oars and crept down among the blankets to let the boat slowly find its way through the still water. With our gaze turned upwards, we waited for our eyes to get used to the dark and for the sky above to become filled with stars and shooting stars. The August night was chilly, but the water was still warm, so mist formed and crept around the boat. We glided along, as if on a cloud, looking out into the universe. Soon we saw the first meteor burn up, followed shortly by the next, and it didn't take long before it was hard to count them all. We could in principle follow the origin of all the white lines to one and the same area, the constellation Perseus. This meteor shower, which culminates in mid-August each year, has been named the Perseids precisely because of its visible origin in the sky. Sometimes it's also called the Laurentian tears or Saint Lawrence's tears after Saint Lawrence, who died on a red-hot gridiron after having defended the sick and poor before the governor of Rome.

The Swift-Tuttle comet, which drags in its wake Saint Lawrence's tears, was discovered independently by Lewis Swift (1820–1913) and Horace Parnell Tuttle (1837–1923) in 1862. It is believed that a larger piece of the comet detached that year, giving rise to a large amount of debris. The comet is also on the list of possible objects that might collide with earth in the near future, though the risk is seen to be rather slight. Tuttle was otherwise a famous comet hunter in the spirit of Charles Messier, naming many celestial objects. Among other things, he's given his name to the Tempel-Tuttle comet, which we can see in mid-November every year pulling the dust cloud called the Leonids after it. Every thirty-third year, the performance is extra spectacular, being most recently seen at the end of 1999, just before the turn of the millennium.

Just a few metres from the beach at the summer cottage formerly stood a smoker. My grandfather had built it himself to smoke eel in. The lake was full of them, if one is to believe his stories. And they were equally common everywhere, in streams, ditches, wells, rivers, creeks and other lakes. I, myself, have only seen eels at the cottage on one occasion, when I scared up a specimen from the clay bottom as I was out swimming. The homemade smoker is gone, but according to the local fishing association there are eels left in Tolken, which are increasingly rare in our waters.

The eels' journey from inland and through our coastlines to the Sargasso Sea begins in the autumn. They start moving when the moon hangs low in the sky, under the protection of night and with the help of the currents. They go to the mythic birthplace and playground of all eels, far from the Swedish waters. The eels never appear in the light and are generally regarded as mysterious creatures of the dark. My grandfather's fishing trips in the summer evenings were slow, exacting, almost ceremonial. It wasn't the hunt for eels or, even better, zander, that was the really important thing. Just like with the experience of the shooting stars, it wasn't the meteors themselves that gave the lasting memory but the knowledge that there exists something more out there in the dark, something to learn more about or just marvel at. I wonder if my children will be able to take their own children out on the lake.

THE ONLY MOON?

Night starts at 6 degrees after the onset of astronomical twilight. But it's not necessarily completely dark. In the deepest hour of night, the sun still reminds us of its presence, not least through the moon's reflection of its light. The light of the full moon is 400,000 times weaker than the midday sun but quite enough to guide us through the night and have an effect on everything from insects to people. It's no exaggeration to say that the moon has been enormously significant throughout history – culturally, physically and ecologically.

Under a brightly shining moon, toads and frogs don't sing as loudly, and salamanders, beetles and moths forgo their nocturnal escapades. The light of the moon is exposing, and many are the animals that organise their lives by its cycle. Certain bat species, especially those that hunt near trees in clearings or close over the water, seem to possess a moon phobia, probably from an inherited fear of birds of prey and animals lurking beneath the water's surface or in the shrubbery. Other bats fly on as usual. Outside the mine by the Taberg mountain in the Swedish province of Småland, late one evening in summer or early autumn, when the bats swarm in their mating dance and reconnoitre winter dwellings, they do so without any concern for the phases of the moon.

There are plenty of people who claim to be affected by the moon. Particularly common is perceived difficulty sleeping but also disturbed menstruation, anxiety and worrying. Some yoga instructors advise against practising and even cancel their sessions at the full moon, as they think we are too affected by it. In the labour ward at Karlstad Central Hospital, there's a notice board with recorded times for childbirth. On the board, there's also a marker for when the full moon occurs. The reason for this is that there's a widespread myth that more children are born during nights with full moons than nights with new moons. But the board provides a clear message: that's not the case. Children are born at any time.

In the media, you can sometimes read that people are made a little crazy during the full moon and that the police receive more calls then. The concept of lunacy is very much alive, and the moon is behind many modern myths. But research and statistics speak against these beliefs. Madness, accidents and crimes are only perceived to be under the full moon's influence. The number of reported crimes isn't greater during nights with full moons. And as for disturbed sleep, well, that's not about the moon at all. It's the light. A person who experiences worsened sleep in the presence of the full moon maybe simply needs better curtains.

Myths surrounding the moon are, of course, not a modern phenomenon and have held a central position in culture since far back in time. In 2008, the secret behind the Antikythera mechanism – a strange object found in the waters off Greece more than a hundred years earlier – was revealed. It turned out to be a two-thousand-year-old astronomical calendar, whose mechanical system could show the orbit of the sun, of the brightest stars rising and setting, and of all the phases of the moon; it could even predict solar and lunar eclipses. To know when the full moon was approaching was very worthwhile in a world without lights, because transport could run or the army could manoeuvre at night, thanks to its light.

Today, we're uncovering more and more of the secrets of the universe, and it's now been more than fifty years since humanity took its first small steps on the surface of the moon and with them the giant step into the space age. At the same time, more and more astronomical experiences and phenomena are being wiped out for ordinary people. In the illuminated skies of big cities, where we can hardly see any stars anymore, there's still the visible moon, and it moves in the same path, following the same rhythm as in the generations before us. It secretly hides its rear side, showing only its illuminated face and those flecks that throughout the ages have given rise to fantasies about child abduction and divine punishment.

In the novel *1Q84*, Japanese author Haruki Murakami writes about an alternative world with an extra moon in the heavens. Whether this novel might have been the inspiration for a current Chinese project I will leave unsaid, but the extra moon can now become a reality. In Chengdu, in southwest China, an effort is under way to avoid once and for all inconvenient and expensive street lighting. Instead, a private space research institute wants to send up an artificial moon. The extra moon in the form of a satellite will be precisely programmed in its orbit around the earth so that it constantly follows Chengdu with its eight million inhabitants and illuminates streets and squares by reflecting sunlight at night. The slightly crazy project has of course been met with a lot of scepticism, but in 2018, the English-language *China Daily* wrote that Chinese engineers are planning three more artificial moons to put into orbit, which is expected to save one billion dollars in energy costs annually. The light from each moon is about eight times stronger than the original moon's light and is equivalent to the kind of light found a little into twilight. As in Murakami's novel, this will change the experience of night itself and also the conditions for millions of humans, animals and plants.

Not even on a moonless night is the sky completely without the indirect impact of the sun. Along the ecliptic – the path of the sun's perceived orbit around the earth – light rays are reflected by space dust and form a faint, ghostly glow, called *zodiacal light*. The space dust, consisting of micrometre-sized particles from meteors and comets, generates a triangular shimmer against the underlying starry sky, and during a clear night with a new moon, the zodiacal light constitutes about 60 per cent of the light. The light is often depicted as a cone, like a spotlight on a dark theatre stage. And there are many people out walking at night who've been deceived into believing that it is dawn, which is why the zodiacal light is also called *false dawn*. The phenomenon was scientifically described by the astronomer Giovanni Domenico Cassini in the seventeenth century but has, of course, been known since the earliest days of mankind. In early Muslim texts, from the very era of Muhammad himself, devout Muslims are warned about the wolf's tail, the false dawn which appears as a vertical light in the night sky. During Ramadan, when meals can only be eaten between dusk and dawn, it's particularly important to keep that concept in mind. The real dawn arrives in the form of horizontal light and not at all like the heavenly wolf tail.

But in our modern world, where glowing city skies eat into the night, it's not the wolf's tail that we should fear, but mankind's false dawn.

THE BLUE MOMENT

I'm sitting on the bus on the way out of Gothenburg, Sweden. Along with other passengers, lone truck drivers and people driving cars, I form part of a huge, winding line down National Road 40. As the road curves, the light shines from thousands of red lights against the dark blue sky. In the other direction, I'm met by white headlights, slightly sparser but in a constant stream. The newer the cars, the whiter and brighter the light. Further out from the city, the line slowly thins out, and soon it's just fragments of the coiling worm remaining. When the bus turns off shortly thereafter, I see the valley, and we approach the hills that make up the town of Bollebygd where I live. Hundreds of yellow pinpricks, like in a scattered pointillist painting, create increasingly dense formations, but most can be discerned as individual homes. In the seemingly opaque darkness outside the bus window, it's hard to see how these small dots of light could actually pollute the darkness. But the number grows and grows, and soon some of them can't be separated. If you look upwards, you can see that the sky is dimly fluorescent. That's the clouds reflecting the light that the houses in the city centre give off. I get off at the school, it's Saint Lucia's Day, and above me the Geminids are raging by in one of the massive meteor storms that we can experience here on earth. But I don't see them. In the haze of the car park lights, only raindrops can be seen. The weather and the lights are effectively blocking the spectacle. But the Geminids tend to be bigger every year, and I hope I can see to it to be in a darker place with clearer weather next Saint Lucia's Day, and so get to take part in the captivating spectacle.

Just before Lucia in 2016, I was invited to Korpilombolo in the Pajala municipality in Norrbotten, northern Sweden. On the way there, the December sun made a fleeting attempt to light up the ice over the Gulf of Bothnia but soon gave up again. The onward journey north via Överkalix took two hours, and to a person from further south in Sweden, it seemed incredibly exotic, with place names written in a Finnish dialect called Meänkieli, with the crusty, frozen landscape and the black sky. Once there, I could almost feel that I was touching the Arctic Circle, and an abundant snowfall began.

I was there to talk about the bat's nocturnal life at the Korpilombolo community centre during the fortnight-long night festival, an annual event in the village in December, during which the slightly more than five hundred inhabitants go outside, instead of trying to escape the darkness, and meet up under the black sky accompanied by relatives, returning residents and friends, but also by curious visitors from the southern part of the country, like myself. The local restaurants come to life with candles and music, the sky feels clearer than ever before and the sledge tracks between the shops, the church, the homes and the parks don't even have time to be re-covered by snow in between trips because there are so many people walking about.

Poets and speakers mingle with musicians, artists and craftsmen, all of it happening in the spirit of darkness and night. In the far north, people don't mourn the summer. The winter may be harsh, but it is a part of the people's soul.

The phenomenon in which the sun never rises during the day is usually referred to as 'polar night'. In Finnish, it is called *kaamos* – a constant darkness, a long, uninterrupted night. It may sound gloomy and melancholy, but with the word also comes calm. There's not too much to do during that period, or at least there hasn't been, historically. So it's been permissible just to be, to sleep, to philosophise and to have conversations.

Kaamos is like the hibernation of the plants before they stretch out towards the light again in spring. But it is actually not completely dark. Stars light up the sky like Christmas decorations, and the northern lights come by now and then with nature's own neon and laser play. Green, purple, vibrant. I've experienced it myself once in my life, a relatively faint occurrence but still fully visible and surprising. I was standing watch in the Norrland night, far above the High Coast, looking out into the darkness. It was one of the many field exercises of my military service, and I had the rotation during the early-morning hours, when a slow pulse of light suddenly rose over the horizon.

With growing and then waning intensity, green and pale violet at the edges, the lights rose up over me like gauzy, fluttering curtains and flashed faintly in slow motion. Maybe I wouldn't have seen this spectacle if I hadn't already been staring out into the pitch darkness below for an hour. My night vision had had time to develop, rhodopsin had built its molecular stacks and opened my retinas to the weakest of light. It took me a moment to understand that I was standing under the northern lights, *aurora borealis*. Although it was just a hint of what the grander northern lights can be, I remember it clearly as a powerful display.

Polar lights – northern lights in the north and the southern lights in the south – arise when the solar winds reach the earth's atmosphere at an altitude of 16 kilometres. Electrons, charged particles, fall towards the earth in oval formations at the poles, controlled by the earth's magnetic field. At the northern latitudes, we call it the Auroral Oval. The higher the solar activity and the warmer the currents of electrons from the solar winds, the further from the poles we can see the effects. Normally, we can perceive the northern lights during dark winter nights in the northernmost parts of Scandinavia, in northern Canada and in Siberia. Viking tales speak of the northern lights as reflections of the Valkyries' armour when they led warriors to Odin in his preparations for Ragnarök.

In rare cases, we can see the polar lights in southern Sweden as well, far from the cities. But it takes thick darkness for the dancing electron winds to offer their spectacular light phenomenon. Under the grey-yellow city skies we have to make do with knowing what's out there; we can never see it with our own eyes.

The polar darkness also offers other nuances. There's a blue colour that settles like a weak filter across the vastness, especially in the afternoon. If you look south, you'll see a faint redness from the hidden sun, while the landscape to the north is a deep blue rather than black. In the middle of the day, the blue light takes over and even the snow seems like something painted by Edvard Munch. *Kaamos* has become synonymous with the blue hours in the middle of the day that culminate in *the blue moment*, when it feels as if the entire landscape is immersed in a swimming pool and then abruptly plucked out again. The short moment of blue is the winter's own twilight and can be experienced only at the edge of the Arctic Circle, particularly before the winter solstice has arrived. As I learnt, one must wish to peer into the dark night to see the mysterious and beautiful light that it holds.

YELLOW-GREY SKY

Following an earthquake in Los Angeles in 1994, the city was hit with a major power outage. Neighbourhood after neighbourhood went dark, and instead, the stars began to reappear in increasing numbers above the rooftops. The local emergency services centre was said to have got calls from anxious people wondering about the strange light phenomenon appearing in the heavens – the Milky Way, which hadn't been seen in Los Angeles for decades. The stories are, of course, a bit exaggerated, but they still show how unusual it is for us city-dwellers today to see stars properly, and of course astronomers were grateful to tell the story. How many people actually called the police is unclear; however, the director of the Griffith Observatory answered the phone several times that evening.

The observatory is located in Griffith Park, Los Angeles, a slightly wilder equivalent of New York's Central Park. Here there are well-attended exhibitions covering the various aspects of astronomy, and no fewer than seven million people have looked through the eyepiece on the Zeiss telescope since 1935, even though it has been a long time since anyone could really see stars in Los Angeles. But despite the city lights, you can still see the surface of the moon, our neighbouring planets and the brighter objects of the heavens.

The Gothenburg city observatory, Slottsskogen Observatory,

has had its scope turned towards the sky since 1929, and when Halley's Comet gave Sweden temporary space-fever in the mid-1980s, the facility was expanded to its current size. These days, the Gothenburg astronomy club meets from time to time in the observatory kitchenette for a snack, while in the dark of the exhibition hall yet another ancient model of the starry sky glitters. Above all, each time the roof is opened to the side and the telescope is brought to life, it's still cause for a small moment of celebration in the observatory. Because even if the city sky outside isn't quite as black today, it's breathtaking to see the roof open up to space and the telescopic lens directed towards the unknown. The darkness falls slowly down through the ceiling and soon occupies the entire space where the telescope is standing. The observatory becomes one with the universe.

Halley's Comet appears once in a human lifetime, every seventy-sixth year, and is next expected in 2061. The question is whether, by that time, there will be an observatory left in Gothenburg that can capture any emerging interest in space. The Andromeda Galaxy and most of the stars have long since disappeared in the fiery yellow haze above the big city. Only one of five people in Europe can see the Milky Way on a daily basis, and in North America and Europe, nearly everyone, 99 per cent, lives under a sky affected by artificial light. Few people know real darkness or what a starry sky looks like. It's almost impossible to imagine the night that was commonplace for mankind only a couple of generations ago.

The painting *Starry Night* by Vincent van Gogh (1853–90) is one of history's most famous depictions of a living night sky. It dates back to a time just before the electric light took over the cityscape, when the natural night with its star fireworks was public property. It's easy to interpret the painting's swirling depictions of stars in blue and yellow as chaos and madness, especially as van

Gogh at this time had been admitted to the sanatorium in Saint-Rémy-de-Provence in France. Like many artists, he was affected by the black bile, as they used to refer to it – the creative depression; melancholy that was attributed by Aristotle to artists, philosophers and poets. The myth of artists' inherent darkness has a long history. For the sake of his health, van Gogh chose to spend a year at a sanatorium in the South of France where he created many of his most famous paintings, of which *Starry Night* is one in a line of night motifs. Maybe this was a manifestation of his inner darkness, or simply of how the night sky could be experienced as crackling and chaotic – at least before the arrival of electric lighting.

Sweden's most famous night artist would be Eugène Jansson (1862–1915), whose paintings of Stockholm at night show the time just before the breakthrough, when only a few streets had been reached by electric lights. It's a brief moment in history in which the old and the new meet. Jansson's paintings are often painted in dark blue tones with reflections of faint gas lamps in water, lamps that are now long absent from the streets of Stockholm.

In London, 1,500 gas lamps still spread their light, as a remnant from the time when it was mandatory for lanterns to be lit in the city between All Saints' Day and Candlemas Day. From Buckingham Palace along the Mall to Covent Garden, the old lights are still lit every night, for no other reason than aesthetics and nostalgia. The oldest functioning lamps are those from the late eighteenth century. Until 1976, the gas lamps were lit manually using a flame on the end of a 2.5-metre-long brass rod, but now they light automatically. It takes a lot of work to keep the lights burning, and they need to be inspected and adjusted every fortnight so that their faint, homely glow can continue to tame the twilight. Although the gas lamps belong primarily to the Victorian era and soon came to be replaced by electric lights, their legacy is nurtured in London. The royal family is particularly concerned with this heritage, which is why contemporary gas lamps are set up around the palace instead of electric lights.

Electricity is without a doubt one of man's most revolutionary discoveries and has fundamentally changed the way we live. Thomas Alva Edison (1847–1931) received a patent in 1880 for a commercially available light bulb, and with that we entered a new era in human history. Let there be light, or, as it said on a poster for Blanch's Café in Stockholm at the end of the nineteenth century, 'Electric Lighting in the evening'.

INDUSTRIAL LIGHT

My grandfather's father and my namesake, Johan Eklöf, grew up contemporaneous with the short era of gas lamps and the emergence of industrial Sweden. He was born in Madängsholm in the municipality of present-day Tidaholm, whose proximity to the Tidan River and its rushing waters made it a perfect place for industry. His ancestors had worked in the quarries in the black Cambrian shale, where I myself looked for fossils in the late 1990s. There was a mill that had stood there since the eighteenth century and eventually a sawmill and a dyeing and a wool factory. Johan Eklöf started his work at the wool mill at only twelve years old, in 1878. He started work at six o'clock in the morning and finished at eight o'clock in the evening, except during the most urgent times in the autumn when the working day lasted until ten. In the winter, you also had to come in earlier, maybe at five o'clock, to start firing and getting up the heat. The factory didn't take into account light and darkness, seasons or sleep cycles. Inside the mill, there was constant darkness. Johan longed for the light and the natural rhythm of the sun, so on Sundays he went along with arranged pleasure trips to Tidaholm and Jönköping, where there was socialising and accordion music.

Two decades later, he'd worked his way up and been honoured with the title of 'spinning master' in the region's new scutching and weaving mill. But he had no greater privileges. Admittedly, the salary was quite good at 100 kronor a month, but when he wanted a day off to marry my pregnant great-grandmother, Jenny, his employer said no. The proposed wedding date was the same day as the salary payments and the spinning master was therefore required to wait a week. No one else could have handled that job.

During Johan's early days as a spinning master, he first grew acquainted with electric lighting. In 1895, the first wires were pulled into the factory, which was early compared to many other places in the country. Before that, both the offices and factory floors had been lit by paraffin lamps, a very dim light that was made dimmer still by all the dust in the premises.

The new electric lighting was expensive, and, for financial reasons, no lights were permitted to be stronger than sixteen normal lights – that is to say sixteen wax candles. Taking the Swedish Work Environment Authority's current recommendations into account, we can state that this standard didn't meet our modern requirements. We would have found what was then considered an illuminated industrial space rather dark. In the old days, at the end of 1940s, my great-grandfather was interviewed for a newspaper article about what it was like to work in the textile industry around the turn of the century, and he said, among other things: '. . . I just wonder, what the safety representative or whatever it's called would say, if our factories today have that sort of lighting.'

The change had only just begun. Mankind had ever so slowly started to create a world where day and night were one and the same. In time, with improved industrial working conditions, other kinds of businesses followed suit. Shops were open longer, the range of entertainment increased, the light from shopfronts and eventually televisions spread out through the growing town centres, and like moths to a flame, people were drawn to the cities. The future was bright, or at least, brightness was the future.

Mankind's lifelong dream of defeating the darkness was about to be realised, and there were few people who reflected that light could be harmful; on the contrary, we had everything to gain from lighting the lamp of industriousness in every home.

In pre-industrial society, night was considered the evil time of the day, as the dark hid all kinds of devilry. But defenders of the darkness have always existed. Some of Europe's learned priests believed that the night was as holy as the day, for God had intended it so. The idea was that humans should simply stay at home, pray, and take care of their obligations, not be out in the shadows. As early as 1662, a London-based priest is believed to have said: 'We won't make day of night, nor night of day.'

During the Enlightenment, the author Jean-Jacques Rousseau (1712–78) wrote that God had not given his approval for street lighting. Rousseau stood strong as a critic for the ideals of the Enlightenment and believed that mankind risked losing its soul in an overly artificial world. The astronomers in late-nineteenth-century Paris and London also advocated for natural darkness when they noticed that the zodiacal light and the faint stars disappeared when the smog of the city was lit by the glow of gas lamps. They were supported by the obsessively opinionated August Strindberg (1849–1912), who was not very optimistic about the introduction of the electric lights. In 1884, during his time in Switzerland, he wrote 'On the General Dissatisfaction, Its Causes and Cures', in which he goes after everyone who believes that the inventions and improvements of modern times are for anyone other than the social elite. Strindberg contended that electric lighting was just another way to get the ordinary worker to work more. And besides, it could hardly be good for the eyes. He writes: 'They talk about telephones, consumer associations, higher wages, oil paintings, and easier communication, they point to banks (which didn't fail), charities (with pietism and humiliation), about electric light (which destroys the eyes and lengthens the working day – for the worker), as if not all this were mere expressions of a feverish pursuit of betterment.'

Strindberg was partially correct that lighting was political. It was, of course, a way to increase efficiency, but it was also a demonstration of strength, in the same way as were the striking installations and the presentations of candles in the eighteenth century. Light could project wealth and power. The darkness could be dispelled with the light, and everyday life changed for ordinary people. Work was to be done within the mills, and around the mills the city grew. And the city never sleeps.

WHEN THE CLOCKS ARE OFF

Looking at a contemporary tropical metropolis from a distance, it's as though daylight gets sucked in and absorbed by the city centre sometime around 6 pm. At the same time as darkness settles over the surrounding landscape, the city begins to radiate light in all directions, as if the sun had never set behind the horizon but instead parked inside the city centre. The countless lights in the city seem to form a single shining defence against the surrounding night.

At other latitudes with clearer seasonal changes – like, for example, in northern Sweden – you don't see the same distinct contrasts during the summer. Dusk seems to go on until dawn, and the city light is less conspicuously spread out into general dimness. As winter approaches, however, you can see a phenomenon here, similar to that in the tropical cities. In the north, the snow has always reflected the northern lights, starlight and moonlight and brightened up the long nights of winter. These days, the snow reflects light from streetlamps and headlights instead, and a German study has measured the extent to which this occurs. Different places in the world were compared – Berlin's suburbs, a beach on the Baltic Sea in Latvia, and Rovaniemi municipality, north of the Arctic Circle in Finland – and it turned out that snow-covered streets reflect streetlights and illuminate the sky with 33 per cent more light than areas with neither snow nor artificial lighting. If it's cloudy, the artificial light is reflected back to the ground and the experience within the city is as if we had a double full moon every night. The downward-facing, shielded lights that are sometimes recommended to minimise light scattering work less well when there's snow lying on the ground.

Further south, like in my own old hometown of Gothenburg, you could probably say that we measure snow in duration rather than depth. In winter, we move along sepia-toned streets, as if in a colourised, blurred photograph. The yellow streetlights are reflected in even the smallest drop of water, creating a grey-orange mist just in time for the period of the year when the Liseberg amusement park is usually decorated with matching pumpkins. Many people say that they get depressed in the constant darkness of the hazy west coast, while others like the opportunities the season offers to escape under a blanket without a guilty conscience. I can't help thinking about how we would have reacted if the city proposed real darkness instead of all these shades of grey-yellow. Would we have felt better or worse?

On the cusp of spring in Gothenburg – and maybe everywhere throughout Sweden – a phenomenon occurs that has caused many foreign visitors to take note. At bus stops, along south-facing walls, on streets and on squares, people stop, turn their heads up towards the sky and stand quietly for a moment. It seems almost religious, though their eyes are seeking not God but the very oldest of gods, the sun. When the sun's rays hit our skin, the body produces vitamin D, a substance that, among other things, helps us to make use of calcium and so strengthens our bones. People staying in the dark for long periods of time risk not getting the amounts of natural vitamin D that we need, and maybe we feel that when we instinctively turn towards the sun. Our bodies simply require the strong sunshine at a chemical level.

The bright blue and violet rays of the sun during the day don't just help the body to produce vitamin D. As soon as our retinas are hit by the morning's sun, photons cause signals to be sent via the nerves to the *suprachiasmatic nucleus* – a junction of the brain that is the centre of the circadian rhythm. From here, among other things, the pineal gland, which is responsible for the body's sleep hormone, *melatonin*, is controlled. Melatonin is transported via blood and spinal fluid out to the cells. Daylight keeps the levels of melatonin at a low level, and we feel active and alert. When natural outdoor light decreases and changes colour, the amount of melatonin increases. Humans, just like other animals and plants, too, react differently to different types of light. The blue light means it's day, the red means it's evening. Of course, it's more complicated than that, but more than anything the bluish daylight resets our internal clock through the cryptochromes, the light-sensitive proteins, and indicates that the day can begin again.

Our built-in food and sleep clocks follow, just like the clock, a daily cycle of about twenty-four hours. But the fact is that most of us have a cycle that runs a little longer, about fifteen minutes extra. If the inner clock is allowed to tick along freely, we'll slowly shift our day, which has been proven with people who've been trapped in the dark for a long time as well as people who are completely blind. So, blindness can also be accompanied by sleep difficulties or just difficulty living in the same rhythm as the rest of society, because the body feels completely natural resting a little bit later every day. And before you know it, it's the middle of the night. Some people have a somewhat shorter rhythm, and they are typically morning people.

For many animals, in addition to adapting to the shifts in time of day, it's also important to prepare for hibernation or the arrival of spring. Melatonin also plays a major role there. Long periods of high levels of melatonin indicate that it's winter, and vice versa, shorter periods of the sleep hormone mean that the days have got longer and lighter. Then, it's spring, with completely different conditions.

Between sunset and midnight, there is a steady rise in the levels of the sleep hormone, which triggers a variety of reactions in the body. We get tired, and the body prepares for the night's sleep cycles, brain recovery and the processing of the day's impressions. Body temperature drops, metabolism decreases and we become less hungry. The latter point is due to melatonin triggering another hormone, namely *leptin*, which tells us what our energy stores are like and how we should manage them. During the night, the leptin content rises, to sink again after sunrise. Leptin follows in the wake of the melatonin waves and regulates our appetite, rhythmically and regularly. This was of course particularly important in the earliest days of mankind, when we needed to conserve energy and couldn't go out looking for food in the middle of the night. It was only in the morning that the body told us that it was time to eat.

In the age group of fifteen to twenty-nine-year-olds, more than 80 per cent of people have their phones with them in bed. The last thing we do in the evening is set an alarm, check social media, read emails or just scroll. Before that, we might have spent a couple of hours in front of the television or the computer, followed by a few minutes in a bright, white-tiled bathroom. Maybe we had an evening snack because the effects of leptin, the hormone that makes us feel full, hadn't kicked in. When we finally turn everything off and close our eyes, we can still sense the streetlights outside the window. Passing cars may occasionally light up the room, or the neighbour's garden lighting peeks in from behind the curtain. No matter what light we expose ourselves to in the evening, we're disturbing the natural wave of melatonin, which is meant to wash over us at dusk, eventually ebbing away in time for the morning. The worst is the blue light, which is most similar to daylight, but other light affects us, too.

At Harvard University, it's been shown that light values of eight lux are sufficient to interfere with our melatonin cycle. The light value corresponds to that in the evening, the civil twilight. The disturbance means that we don't get sleepy at the right time, the brain and body don't slow down, the metabolism continues as usual and we get hungry when we shouldn't. Our quality of sleep is getting worse. Is anyone surprised?

SICK WITH LIGHT

That poor-quality sleep has a huge effect on us isn't news. Anyone who's taken care of small children, worked a night shift, flown across several time zones or been out clubbing for a full night can attest to that. Exhaustion can be devastating, but at the same time, it's easy enough to address, at least in normal cases. A good night's sleep and the body is renewed. Recurring sleep problems, however, can lead to chronic stress and depression, and even physical ailments as a result. The body enters a vicious circle where stress and disturbed sleep go hand in hand. We become vaguely depressed. Today, tens of millions take some form of antidepressants – depression is quite simply a public health crisis. We may not be able to cure or prevent depression all at once by cutting down on electric lighting, but we definitely increase the chances of a good sleep in the long run.

To achieve this, we can resort to various tricks: some people like to sleep in an environment where the natural light calibrates their interior clock, others simply prefer to have it as dark as possible throughout their sleep at night. The important thing is that the light varies during the day and the waves of melatonin levels can come and go at a regular rate. Blue light during the day, red in the evening.

In addition to stress, depression and sleep problems, obesity is also a global health problem. Of course, there are many causes, but one of these is constant low leptin levels, which are a direct result of the breaking of the melatonin circle. We fatten ourselves with light, simply put. But it doesn't stop there; melatonin also controls other hormones and processes that are important for our immune system. When the Danish researcher Johnni Hansen examined seven thousand women with breast cancer twenty years ago, he was able to draw an important conclusion: night shifts increase the risk of tumour formation. Hansen's work has been replicated over and over again. Nurses, flight crews and factory workers, who work night shifts and are awake at night more often than the rest of us, run a greater risk, statistically, of suffering from a cancerous disease at some point. This seems to be especially true of hormone-sensitive cancers such as breast and prostate cancer. The World Health Organization has gone as far as to classify night shifts as a real cancer risk in the same category as smoking.

The causal relationships are definitely not simple, but part of the explanation lies in the night illumination. It's known that, among other things, melatonin and its effect on other hormones contributes to the inhibition of tumours, and if the biological clock is disturbed in such a way that the melatonin wave is absent at night, the positive effects are decreased and cancer tumours are at greater risk of growing.

Researchers in Israel have found a link between disease rates and the amount of short-wave blue light present at night. In the most light-polluted parts of the country, hormone-sensitive cancers such as breast cancer were more common, while lung cancer, for example, was not. We still don't know everything about how light affects us humans and the extent to which a disturbed sleep cycle causes different kinds of health issues. But it is clear that night workers are more at risk than other people. In our modern society, however, it is difficult to avoid night shift work completely. Key functions depend on the availability of staff around the clock. At Karlstad Central Hospital (the hospital with the birth chart showing the full moon), the municipality has invested heavily in modern lighting. The lights are governed by the time of day, mimicking natural diurnal variation. In the middle of the day, the light is white, with a large proportion of blue wavelengths. As the evening progresses, blue light decreases in favour of redder shades, just as it would during natural sunset. The intensity also varies, from a faint, dawn-like light that slowly becomes more intense between morning and afternoon and then gets more and more subdued again. Night lighting in all areas of the hospital also depends on what's going on. Where there is no need for bright light, there's simply no light. The lights are set so that night staff can do their work in the light, but the light is without the blue component entirely. The daytime running lights are pre-programmed, but they can be adjusted as needed. Patients are said to sleep better, as are the staff once they get off their shifts. Karlstad's model, which is also used in other places, shows that we can regulate the amount of light as well as its colour in order to meet our needs for both light and darkness. Now the only thing left is to transfer these technologies into more environments where mankind's light activity endangers human health.

PART IV: IN PRAISE OF SHADOWS

LIKE A BALM FOR THE SOUL

One might conceivably wonder why a book about darkness has been as much about light as this one has, and I've asked myself that question as I've worked on it. But in the texts that I've come across on the subject, darkness is only defined by light. Darkness is seen, quite simply, as an absence of light, in the same way that an absence of sound is often used to define silence. According to this approach, darkness is a kind of primordial state, ceasing to be darkness at the very moment when visible light is present.

I've been guilty of this myself, having used such a definition on several occasions, yet it is my absolute view that darkness has an independent worth. For one thing, it can be as concrete to our senses as light. It can creep over us; it can be overwhelming, restful or frightening. If we were in a room completely without light, we probably would not describe it just as dark but maybe as pitch-black or coal-black. In the same way, a room lit by a candle isn't perceived as particularly bright, but rather as dark or at least semi-dark. Although, by strict definition, it's light that can be measured, the subjective experience is often marked by the darkness. Darkness can fall, it can be intrusive and dense. 'The intrusion of darkness', we say, as if its proximity is an assault on our existence. Emotionally and linguistically, darkness is something substantive and tangible. We use words such as 'obscure' and 'murky' to describe a darkness between completely light and completely dark – in a literal but also in a moral or metaphorical sense. The journalist Åke Lundqvist once wrote: 'Darkness is not the absence of light. Light is diluted darkness. The speed of light is often talked about, in a kind of admiration. The speed of darkness is much slower, darkness falls softly and quietly, as a balm for the soul.'

So, darkness is a phenomenon in its own right, I posit, yet it still seems infinitely more difficult to define than light. Especially without using light as the opposite pole. In our lived world the two seem forever connected, therefore a book about darkness must also inevitably be about light and not least about the interplay between light and darkness. Because without light, no darkness, and without darkness, no light.

In many mythologies, the relationship between light and darkness is about just this subject. The two are united but also each other's opposite poles. The night is the mother of the day, as the poet Johan Stagnelius (1793–1823) wrote, referring to the Nordic goddess of mythology, Natt ('Night'), who was the mother of Dag ('Day'), Jord ('Earth'), Sol ('Sun') and Måne (Moon). In most creation stories around the world, darkness and night are the original chaos, while day and light symbolise life and its origin; a sun god enters, Mother Earth takes shape. We recognise this theme from the Bible:

'In the beginning God created the heaven and the earth. And the earth was without form, and void; and darkness was upon the face of the deep. And the Spirit of God moved upon the face of the waters. And God said, Let there be light: and there was light. And God saw the light, that it was good: and God divided the light from the darkness. And God called the light Day, and the darkness he called Night. And the evening and the morning were the first day.'

God not only evokes the light but is the light and all that is good in the world. In his dwelling – the church – the rooster reigns as a symbol of dawn, which is the moment when the night is defeated. Darkness is the absolute opposite of light and the antithesis of God: the devil, death, ignorance and all the despair in the world. The prophet Isaiah, who was a bit of a pessimist, preached about life without God. He writes, among other things: '. . . distress and darkness and night of anxiety. Yes, thick darkness is the life of the displaced.'

Man is said to be blind without light, literally as well as in the theological sense. Only by trusting in the light that God stands for can we get out of darkness, resist temptation and flee evil. This view has of course affected how we look at the darkness; as recently as April 2020, Pope Francis wrote that when we live in sin we are like human bats. We stay in the dark because the light reveals what we don't want to see, and when the eyes get used to darkness, we no longer recognise the light. The Christian light and the symbolism of darkness thus lives on to the highest degree.

In the magnificent library Biblioteca Medicea Laurenziana in Florence, Michelangelo's bat sculptures guard its dark staircase. The lack of light in the hall was a conscious architectural choice, for it was only when the visitor reached the books that they would be rewarded with light. Before that, they were like bats, uneducated and blind to knowledge. Today's visitors, however, miss out on this well thought-out finesse, as the stairs, in the name of security, are outfitted with lights. But the bats remain there.

The library was built in the sixteenth century under the charge of Pope Clement VII (1478–1534), who had been born into the influential Medici family, which dominated Florence's trade and politics for a few hundred years. Among other things, the family helped to establish contact with China, whose habits, customs and culture differed significantly from those in Europe. In

China, bats, for example, were never regarded as creepy or as images of the ineducable. Instead, they were symbols of happiness, wealth and long life. If you study the statue of Lorenzo II de Medici outside the Medici chapel, also sculpted by Michelangelo, you'll see a small box with a bat on one knee, inspired by Chinese mythology.

In traditional China, darkness and light are two balancing forces of one and the same entity. Light is born from darkness; darkness overtakes light every night. This is a milder form of opposites, where one is dependent on the other. In Nordic mythology, the darkness of the underworld takes over the Nordic autumn but creates life in fresh soil every spring. It's a cycle often attributed to the gods that recurs in religion after religion. It is a rhythm to which man has always subordinated himself, all the way up to modern times, when light pollution slowly but surely has begun to erect walls against the falling of darkness and mandatory rest. Life's renewal every morning and every spring has lost a little of its magic.

IN PRAISE OF SHADOWS

In the 1930s, the Japanese author Junichiro Tanizaki (1886–1965) published *In Praise of Shadows*. By then, the neon age had begun in the world's large cities. Colourful billboards dominated the cityscape and the zeal for illumination had taken a giant first step into the future. Tanizaki was concerned. Japan had a long cultural history with its own architectural identity, and Western influences were starting to take over more and more of the city. The urban landscapes of that time differed a lot from our modern ones. The cities were still relatively dark during the nights, but already at that time, Tanizaki held that we were chasing away the detail and the impressions of history in architecture, smudging out all nuances into one grey mass.

The little book *In Praise of Shadows* has become a classic, especially within the architectural world, and the author himself, Junichiro Tanizaki, was favoured by Harry Martinson, a member of the Swedish Academy, for the Nobel Prize in the 1960s. Tanizaki's musings have laid the foundations for their own school of thought, which has led to Tokyo turning off all the lights in the Roppongi Hills district. They've simply started from scratch with new light sources. Designers have worked with low light intensity, fewer and lower lampposts, soft light on facades, and artworks made out of pleasant lighting. Because the eye always adjusts to the brightest point in its visual field, we tend to experience everything else as darker. One single light or spotlight in a housing block causes the eye to adjust to that level of illumination. Only the retina's cone cells are working, as though it were day. The rod cells are deactivated and so is our night vision. The surroundings around the strong light turn black; we experience a deeper darkness than we would have done without the strong light. One single bright point can completely trick the eye.

In Roppongi Hills, efforts have been made to preserve the darkness as much as possible, making it visible and safe by working with low-intensity and varied illumination. The city is very different when there are no dazzling lights and the skyline is accentuated rather than disappearing into a yellow haze. Light is being filtered, reflected and dimmed. Shadows are alive and create a friendly and inviting darkness that comes to life in its entire muted colour scale.

Junichiro Tanizaki represents an older, Eastern view of life where subtle details and shadows, like the barely discernible texture and patina of different materials, constitute important parts of the full experience. Light and darkness don't oppose each other; it's the nuances that unite the elements in art, architecture and literature. A shadow falling on a tapestry highlights the craft, and golden curtains resting in the semi-darkness generate a different nuance than in exposing light. Often, it is the incompleteness and the transience in natural things that constitutes their beauty, which can be juxtaposed with the generally more distinct striving of the West towards light, clarity and perfection. A significant episode in the book is Tanizaki's praise of the old Japanese toilet:

'[I]t's as if [traditional] Japanese toilets are made for giving peace of mind. They are always placed some distance away from the main building in the shade of a grove where it smells of fresh leaves and moss . . . and it is an indescribable feeling to sit curled up in the semi-daylight sunk deeply into meditation in the feeble light.'

Although the traditional Japanese soul lives on in both architecture and art, it is difficult to find a more technology-oriented city in the world than Tokyo. There, the Japanese countryside feels far away, and it would take many Roppongi Hills to fight the pervasive light pollution.

The absolute contrast of the expansive Tokyo cityscape would be the desolate deserts in the shadow of the Andes on the other side of the Pacific Ocean. The Chilean Atacama Desert is considered to be one of the darkest places on earth, and it's no coincidence that one of the first in a series of conferences held on darkness and the effects of artificial light took place there in 2012. Astronomers, neurobiologists, zoologists and artists visited the symposium and the workshop called Noche Zero. They were all there to discuss the subject of light pollution, which has since become even more acute. The high altitude and clear, dry air of the Atacama Desert – no one knows the last time it rained – constitute an almost optimal spot for stargazing and astronomical research. The observatories have an open view of the cosmos and the infinity of the universe.

Beneath that Chilean starry sky, the perspectives become different. When the eyes' rhodopsin is allowed to build its delicate molecular house of cards without any disturbing lights, the sky opens up. The night offers the entire spectrum of experience and the depth of the starry sky, and nowhere else in the world do you feel so small, so insignificant, and at the same time so unique. The closest stars seem to dip towards the ground, forming a patterned backdrop behind the summits of the Andes. At the same time, the most distant stars light the way towards the beginning of time, like lighthouses on a coast far beyond the Pacific Ocean. Few people realise that this place is not really unique. All these stars are out there no matter where on earth we are. But we have created a blurry barrier, an impenetrable dome over our world, and only in the most remote places can we see beyond the light. Out of all the stars we humans ought to be able to see with the naked eye, for most of us only a fragment, half a per cent, remains. The rest have been absorbed by artificial light, disappeared behind a smokescreen of human activity. They are there, but not there for us to see.

DIODE LIGHT

The incandescent light bulb is history, replaced by the white glow of modern LEDs. Light-emitting diodes, also known as LEDs, take advantage of the fact that atoms are always striving for balance. Adding energy forces an electron further out of the atomic nucleus, after which it soon jumps back and the energy is released again. And this can take the form of photons, i.e. light.

LED light is energy-efficient and can be operated off the grid, using only simple batteries or solar cells. In an LED light, the material from which the diode is made determines what colour the light takes, and for a long time there were only red and green diodes on the market, eventually also yellow. But the physicists Isamu Akasaki, Hiroshi Amano and Shuji Nakamura managed to produce a blue diode and opened up the possibility of developing a strong, white glow, a light that transforms night into day. For this innovation, they were awarded the 2014 Nobel Prize.

By combining modern diodes, light today can be controlled, programmed and set in a way that was never remotely possible with the incandescent light bulb. The LED has revolutionised the market, and the price per lighting unit has fallen sharply, as has energy consumption per unit. The LED lamp has also made light artist and light designer attractive professions. A lot of training has got under way, and every major architectural firm now has lighting as an important part of its business. At first, it was largely about the possibilities for increased power and quantity, as so often is the case with new technology. The actual amount of light had come into focus. But a lot of light and bright light do not necessarily mean that we see better. Sharp lights along our pavements create tunnels of white light, and beyond them we see nothing. We can't see if someone is hiding beyond the light, we don't see the architecture of the city, nor the people moving in the evening. The security aspect gets us to illuminate things to an increasing extent, but the illumination makes us dazzled and blind and – it may well be argued – less secure rather than more.

The human eye is amazing, but it's easy to underestimate its potential in low-light environments and in so doing overestimate the importance of lighting. Imagine a road at night, where the road studs guide you through the darkness. The car's own headlights detail the bends and twists of the road. Then you go through a village. Streetlights take over, shining from above. The experience as you move past the lights is similar to that of a strobe light at a nightclub. Your eyes lose their night vision and their focus; suddenly, the darkness beyond the buildings appears thicker. You hold your breath, wait, and only when you're on the other side of the lighted area can you breathe again. The lights fade and the road is once again visible, stretching before you into the distance, framed only by reflective white lines. The phrase 'less is more' was coined by Ludwig Mies van der Rohe (1886–1969), referring to clean forms in architecture, but it could just as easily refer to lighting. Well-balanced lighting makes it easier for the eye to focus during twilight.

Today, there is the knowledge and the opportunity to design lighting that is adapted for our eyes, that can preserve the nuances of the night, create a vision that goes beyond dazzling lights to shape a harmonious evening experience in urban environments.

LED lights can be directed and in so doing limit how many surfaces are illuminated and reduce unwanted light scattering. It's possible to control and alter the colours to mimic the natural spectrum of daylight, and by controlling the intensity, shadows are accentuated, giving both a more natural and a more pleasant impression.

But over the last decade, we've done just the opposite. We have turned on more and more house lights, headlights, streetlamps, string lights, decorative lights and facade lights. Incandescent bulbs have been replaced by cheaper and more energy-efficient LED lights, but the anticipated energy savings have been eaten up by the sheer number of lights that have been installed. Nor have we taken advantage of the possibilities LED lighting offers in terms of varied intensity; most of them shine brightly and white regardless of location and time. We are blasting ourselves with light.

DARKNESS TOURISM

In our chaotic times, visitors are looking north. There are quiet areas, remote places under open skies and pristine forest areas. The wilder, the better, although at the same time it's nice to be comfortable. Around the world, people are putting together these kinds of experiences in the dark: in Britain, in southern Europe, in national parks in the US, in northern Scandinavia and along the Pacific slopes of the Andes. Astro-tourism – that is, tourism linked to stargazing and the night sky – is on the rise.

One example is Kachi Lodge in Bolivia. At an altitude of 3,660 metres, an hour's flight from the city of La Paz, tourists are offered ancient celestial spectacles. Futuristic, dome-shaped cottages, as you might imagine in a settlement on Mars, are located in the middle of Uyuni, the world's largest salt desert. Inside the white domes, guests sleep as close to the cosmos as one ever can on earth, with an unobstructed view of the starry sky. The restaurant, which is listed in the Michelin guide, serves gourmet domestic dishes, and the barren cactus landscape all around offers the same experience of nature that once inspired the stories of the Inca people.

At the same time as Christopher Columbus sailed west in 1492, paving the way for the European invasion of Latin America, Spain's highest mountain in Tenerife fired off a salute. 'Teide erupted,' Columbus noted in his diary. Columbus devoted no more words than that to the world's third-largest volcano. Today, Teide has been quiet for more than a hundred years, and Tenerife's volcanic area has become both a World Heritage Site and a national park. If you take the cable car up the mountain, you'll travel out into the universe a bit, and the experience of the Milky Way here is more intense than what most people on earth ever approach. As early as the 1960s, observatories were opened on the volcano, and keeping pace with the light spreading from the dense stretches of hotels on the Canary Islands beaches, more and more tourists are looking up to the darkness in search of real night. Astro-tourism has become a billion-dollar industry.

In the Nordic region, we can attract people with the spectacles of the midwinter night, northern lights and stars in sparkling bands. Tourists seek their way to Iceland, Tromsø or Jukkasjärvi's ice hotel to see the sky's own fireworks and have experiences beyond the usual fare. In the middle of the mountain world of Swedish Lapland, one of Europe's oldest national parks, Abisko, is spread out. Here, too, you find darkness and a growing stream of northern lights tourists. As a visitor, you can be guided through the night of the national park with only a dim, red light at hand so as not to disturb your night vision. After a nocturnal ascent in a cable car, you reach STF Aurora Sky Station, where the polar night never seems to end.

But even more everyday experiences are shielded from artificial light in some places. In Helsingborg, to preserve the beautiful sea views even in the evening, lamps on the promenades are adapted so that the view to the west is free from scattered light, and a little bit further south in Lomma, it's written into the city's master plan that dark places have to be preserved.

On Møn, a Danish island southeast of the primary island of Zealand, best known for its spectacular cliffs, nighttime visits have become increasingly popular. The island's 140-metre-high white cliffs are impressively eye-catching in the distance and appear as though they're plunging down into the contrasting waters of the Sound, emerald-green where mountains meet sea. But aside from its white cliffs, Møn is also known for its darkness. On a clear night, five thousand stars can be counted over the island's cliff, which puts Møn high on the Bortle scale, the barometer for astronomical beauty. The corresponding number of stars visible in Copenhagen, just over an hour's drive away, is one hundred. So the entire eastern part of Møn, and parts of the small neighbouring island of Nyord, too, have been made into a reserve – Scandinavia's very first dark park, a nature area that since 2017 has been completely devoted to the unspoiled night. As if that weren't enough, Vordingborg municipality, into which jurisdiction the two islands fall, is also designated a so-called *Dark Sky Community*. This means that the municipality undertakes to safeguard the night and that a strict lighting plan regulates how, where and when there are to be lights. Only the most essential light is allowed.

Møn could have been Swedish land after the peace in Roskilde, when Charles X Gustav completed his legendary march over the Great Belt of Denmark and forced his hereditary enemy to capitulate in 1658. The Swedes' demands were high, but through the negotiation process, the Danes got to keep the islands of Læsø, Anholt and Møn. It's said that the reason for this is that the Danish negotiators had placed beer glasses on the map so that the islands weren't visible. Maybe it was lucky for today's darkness enthusiasts, because the Danish version of the Environmental Protection Agency is a little more advanced than the Swedish in terms of its view of light and darkness.

Even further at the forefront is France, which passed legislation in 2019 on how much light can be emitted into the atmosphere. It remains to be seen how this will be complied with in practice and what the effects will be. But more and more countries are undertaking similar initiatives. In the Austrian capital of Vienna, they've started turning off the lights at 11 pm, and in Groningen in the Netherlands, industry and agriculture lights are regulated by law. Western Europe seems to have woken up in this regard, while the rest of the world is still at the starting block when it comes to the threat of light pollutants.

Møn and Nyord's status as a Dark Sky Community makes them a part of an international movement. Every year, dark parks are certified as special reserves and municipalities of the International Dark-Sky Association (IDA). Only places with extraordinary night skies are even in contention. The areas also need to be reasonably easily accessible by tourists as well as researchers and amateur astronomers. A dark park is intended to be a cultural centre like mediaeval cathedrals and ancient wonders. Unfortunately, there are few places left that meet the IDA's requirements. There are today about forty dark parks and about half as many dark communities worldwide. Only five of them are to be found in Europe, which is why Møn is truly such a unique place.

The dark park on Møn, its stars and the living nocturnal experiences have attracted worldwide attention. During a visit to the park, you can take the opportunity to join one of the many guided tours. On an overcast evening, the experience lies in the darkness itself, in the dense nothingness and its slowly emerging shades as your eyes adjust. The guide presents how best to achieve a sense of security in the dark, how the untrained parts of your sensory apparatus can be activated and how your body responds positively to the visual respite. If the sky is clear, the focus is on the stars. The Milky Way with its sparkling pearls runs the breadth of the heavens, and for those who visit the island in winter, a crackling firework of light from the beginning of time awaits them. Darkness is transformed into a show of lights.

The world's dark parks give hope. There's something uplifting in the fact that it's possible to succeed in preserving parts of the night sky in today's world of technology and illumination – if only we have the will. In Great Britain, there are several dark parks with associated festivals during the spring and winter and around the Halloween weekend, events which attract all kinds of people from across the island kingdom.

The first city to receive Dark Sky Community status was Flagstaff in Arizona, USA, in the year 2001. The city had even then long been a pioneer in this area; as early as 1958, it introduced the world's first lighting regulation, namely a ban on advertising searchlights. Astronomers were the driving force, but the city of Flagstaff developed its own ambition to be able to see the preserved night sky in an urban environment. A model was created where lighting was limited on the basis of three different criteria, similar to those in France's recently established light pollution laws. First, all the lights face downwards and are shielded by upward-facing screens, no light above the horizontal plane allowed. Second, the number of lights in any given area is limited. Third, light from the lamps must be warm; that is to say yellow and red, as opposed to the cold, bluish-white light that affects us most. Flagstaff wants to be a role model and inspire everyone else to dare to follow. If there aren't more cases like Flagstaff, France and Møn and Nyord, we risk having lost the night within a generation.

THE KING'S DARKNESS

At the end of the thirteenth century, Magnus Ladulås, Sweden's then regent, acquired the area that today constitutes southern Djurgården in Stockholm. Since that time, the place has been under royal ownership. For a long time, Djurgården was the court's private hunting grounds, and the word *djurgård* itself refers to *dýr*, the old Norse word for 'deer'. But by the end of the eighteenth century, at the time of King Gustav III, recreation and pleasure rather than hunting took centre stage. The construction of Rosendal Palace in the 1820s was the first of a series of magnificent new buildings, culminating in the inaugurations at the Stockholm Exhibition in 1897. Since then, Djurgården and its surroundings have been dominated by museums, cultural buildings and green parks; it's an outstanding visitor area for both residents and tourists. The next big step was taken in the year 1995. Then the entire area of Ulriksdal-Haga-Djurgården-Brunnsviken was made into a *nationalstadspark*, a protected public area in the city, the first of its kind in the world. The idea was to preserve the combination of history, culture and nature in an otherwise fast-growing metropolis. The project was unique in the world when the decision was made in 1994, but now Sweden has been overtaken by Finland, which has no fewer than ten national city parks.

At the end of the seventeenth century, between Uggleviken and where the Stockholm Olympic Stadium now is, the royal leader of the hunt, Johan Persson – more commonly known as Lill-Jan – had his hunting lodge. Djurgården was rural and wild, and being a hunter for the king meant large tracts of land to monitor. However, the salary wasn't very good. So to increase his income, Lill-Jan opened a restaurant in his house. It quickly became popular, and interest persisted. The restaurant remained long after his death until the nineteenth century. The name Lill-Jan is mentioned in the work of both August Strindberg and Astrid Lindgren, but it was not until 2009 that the forest in the area was officially named after the old hunter and restaurateur. Where Lill-Jan once worked there's still relative darkness, despite all the footpaths and institutions and the proximity to Stockholm's urban crowds. The bats still fly there, too. We've been able to identify seven different species out of the eight that reside in the entirety of Djurgården.

The administration now plans to review the lighting in the area and best adapt it to the needs of both humans and animals. The point of departure is that we need light but also darkness. The bats show the way, and the next step will be to try out modern technology for ecological lighting. So Djurgården and the king become pioneers in Sweden, and the National City Park adds darkness to the list of things to preserve. Maybe we are approaching the idea of creating dark parks similar to that on Møn and Nyord in Sweden, too.

As part of the work at Djurgården, I got the unique opportunity to live in an old market stall at Skansen, a popular open-air museum in Stockholm, and roam freely around the park at night listening to bats. We weren't the only ones who were awake. The normally dozy otters were engaged every night in some sort of convention that seemed to start shortly after sunset and didn't conclude until long after midnight. The wolves slunk around in proud silhouettes, and the mountain owl slowly turned its head in my direction every time I passed the fence. When the wind was blowing from the bay, Skansen was an oasis for bats. Northern bats flew silently along the footpaths and among the protruding heads of the seals, and curious glances from Daubenton's bats followed the caddisflies. Around Hällestadsstapeln, soprano pipistrelles played, and by the Seglora church there circled a male brown long-ear. He'd set up in the steeple hoping that some females would accept his offer of residence. But I saw no females. Skansen is too small an area and far too crammed into a quite illuminated urban landscape to accommodate any larger bat colonies. By all accounts, the brown long-eared male overwinters in Skansen alone, too. But maybe, with a little luck, he will find the company of conspecifics eventually.

Not even Skansen is free from lights and unnecessary spotlights, despite the fact that the park usually closes at dusk. But the lighting is still fairly sparse. The lanterns designed in an earlier era emit a pleasant, dull light, and several walkways are completely darkened. The presence of bats tells us that the city wildlife can still thrive where the water and parks can remain unlit, and hopefully, the whole of Djurgården will eventually come to sing a tribute in praise of the shadows and embrace the Japanese philosophy of the living darkness.

EXTINGUISHED CONVERSATION

A child who was afraid of the dark is said to have remarked, 'It gets lighter when someone's talking.' Loneliness can be more pointed when you can't see anything, and the need for closeness and community becomes stronger. Many people feel insecure in the dark of night and therefore want to have light around them. Our limited night vision has always made it difficult to discern what is out there among the shadows. Even blind people can experience fear of the dark, even though they should, in theory, fare better than anyone else. Just knowing that there's no light or that it's late may be enough for the feeling of being vulnerable to emerge.

Not only can too little light create a sense of perceived insecurity in the darkness, but the wrong kind of light can elicit the same reaction. When we are dazzled by a light, it turns off our entire peripheral field of vision, and darkness creeps in on us from all sides. A row of lanterns along a walkway ensures that we see where we are going, but outside that space lurks a dense nothingness. This is why some lighting designers prefer to talk about darkness, shadows, shades and colour schemes than of lighting, completely in line with the Japanese model from the book *In Praise of Shadows*. The idea is that security and darkness can be experienced together.

Some time ago I signed up for a live art installation, *CONVERSATION*, which sought to find out what happens when we can't see the person we're talking to. You could call it performance art where the participants themselves create the content. The starting point was in part a sociological idea, in which it's you yourself who is meant to converse and listen – not your body, not your gaze – a self freed from prejudices based on appearance. All clear visual expressions become unimportant when the interior self is given free rein.

I was blindfolded, led into a completely darkened room and taken to a place at a table. Soon, I gleaned that we were probably about ten people in the room, maybe more. In front of me was a plate of food, a glass and cutlery. I could smell the food but couldn't see anything at all. The facilitator began by asking us to help ourselves to the food and help each other choose and pour the drinks. Then she let us take over. No one was allowed to say their name, no one was allowed to reveal their profession. It was a bit tentative; someone started a conversational thread that soon died out, and another person commented on the difficulty in knowing which of the two offered drinks he or she actually poured.

Soon the conversation got going, sometimes collectively across the table, sometimes between participants sitting close to each other. Sometimes the facilitator asked us a question, but most of the time she sat quietly. I don't know whether she had any kind of help that let her see us, or if she was also just part of the darkness. There was no obligation to speak, which is why it was difficult to know how many people were there. Maybe some people chose not to reveal their presence, but only listen to the conversations around them.

We took turns guessing what the room around us looked like. At first we imagined a normal conference room, but gradually we ventured out under the starry sky and further down in the deep sea. Our presentations came out slowly, but no one was interrupted in their descriptions. In the absence of visual cues, we all seemed more inclined to wait to the end and let the last of the words land and ebb out before we ourselves or anyone else went on. The voices were distinct even though they were almost whispering, breathing, and the small movements of the chairs were unique to each participant, though barely noticeable.

Could it be that we have forgotten quiet conversation, where silence, darkness and slowness can have their place? Perhaps today it's almost considered a luxury. In psychologists' and therapists' reception areas, it's often lit, but for some patients a dark room would probably be more beneficial. For someone who's hit the wall from stress, a lack of visual stimuli can be soothing. There are psychologists who contend that deeper conversations would benefit from darkness, in which the therapist and the patient could speak undisturbed, completely without other impressions. It is often easier to open up and talk about yourself when you're not visible, not exposed to gazes and scrutiny in a penetrating light.

In any case, I found it novel and valuable to be able to talk like that in the dark, without any reminder of chores and tasks. To be able to listen, talk, be quiet for a while, reflect. Before the time of electric lights, it was in these kinds of circumstances that we spent time together in the evenings and mornings, talking about the past day and maybe telling each other stories. It was possible to sink into a corner of your own and just listen. In a letter to Minze Eisner, a friend he made while convalescing in a sanatorium, Franz Kafka wrote that we hear each other better in the dark. Perhaps we do so because conversation is promoted by the darkness. For me, at least, there was something appealing in not having to be seen during my participation in *CONVERSATION*. I could sit any way I wanted, talk only if I wanted to, but still feel a sense of community with the others.

In peasant society, when the natural light ruled the day, conversations in the middle of the night were part of normal social life. People went to bed early and often woke up for a while at midnight, then went back to sleep a second round until the morning. Many children were conceived that way, during the quiet midnight break. Diaries and other notes tell us that a pipe was often lit, that someone might pick up a simpler bit of handiwork or fill a goblet with beer. A quiet conversation possibly took place before falling asleep again. There are modern studies showing that subjects who follow natural light and sleep cycles soon fall into this biphasic sleep pattern and that it can even be beneficial for health.

The restaurant Svartklubben in Stockholm has taken hold of this concept and made darkness a part of its interior design. Strangers are placed next to each other and unknown voices meet in the completely darkened environment. Hands grope for glasses and silverware, the movements become slow and thoughtful. There are no pauses in the conversation to pick up the phone, as mobiles aren't allowed. The present seems unusually present. Sometimes the restaurateur, who is also a musician, picks up a guitar and plays a bit.

The musicians aren't visible, but you know that they're there. In the dense darkness, every single stanza, every line of text and every harmony appears to create a level of comfort beyond the ordinary. It's been said that many people with ADHD have found themselves at ease at the Svartklubben restaurant and are able to eat, relax and listen without a flood of visual impressions and the passing of time constantly making itself known. Perception of time changes in the dark; the clock seems to slow down and disappear. There's long been talk of light therapy for us northerners in the winter. But the fact is that even dark therapy is starting to become a concept.

In the same area as the restaurant Svartklubben, the podcast *In the dark with* . . . is recorded. The podcast isn't really about darkness, but it's recorded in a dimly lit environment, and the experience of sitting in a room without light is reflected in the conversations; they become deeper, calmer, less stressed and more personal. After a period of acclimation, the guests relax and become themselves. They're not disturbed by any other impressions and can fully focus on what is being said and what they themselves are saying. The listener, of course, doesn't see the darkness, but anyone who closes their eyes can share in the experience.

THE DARKNESS IN THE TUNNEL

Whether it's from the lights at Djurgården, lit oil rigs at sea, Las Vegas hotels or streetlights in Bollebygd's school car park, light pollution affects one of our most basic mechanisms: our inner clock. The circadian rhythm found in all beings on earth changes when the light is on around the clock. Most affected, of course, are the nocturnal animals, but all life is affected.

It is extremely difficult, if not yet impossible, to stop the runaway temperatures on earth, to clean up our environment of plastics and poisons, and to prevent the spread of invasive species – the wrong plants or animals in the wrong places. It's markedly easier to dim or turn off the lights. Light pollution is really the easiest of all the environmental problems to solve, at least technically. The effects of turning off superfluous lighting would be immediate and wouldn't leave behind traces that needed to be cleaned up. We, as private individuals, can, with little cost, reduce our amount of light pollution. With light shades, downward-facing light sources low to the ground and dim lighting, we can reduce cities' total amount of light, as well as the artificial light scattered in the atmosphere. If we turn off lights in rooms we're not in, put timers on our garden lights and motion detectors at the front door, we'll get light when we need it and only when we need it.

Still, of course, the whole thing is far from unproblematic. Light and illuminated environments mean safety for many people, so it may be difficult to accept the increased presence of darkness. There are probably few people who would like to return to the world of pre-industrial lighting. Our conception of our welfare, our security, our professional lives, our way of life and our whole social structure might need to be renegotiated. Light is also a symbol of wealth; in big cities and developed countries it shines the brightest and most often. Just as when Johan Eklöf, my grandfather's father, installed electric lights in the wool mill in the late nineteenth century, and just as when Charles XII was celebrated with thousands of whale oil lamps, lights are a symbol of success. It's hard to refuse an African countryside electric lights when we in Sweden light up our spires and towers with ornamental lighting and drape strands of lights around our trees.

There are several countries and regions that have initiated projects promoting darkness in recent years. In 2002, the Czech Republic and Slovenia were the first in Europe, and several others have followed suit or are well on their way to doing so: Italy, Spain, Croatia, the Netherlands. In many places within the EU, guidelines and possible laws against excessive light and for the preservation of darkness are being discussed.

The question is how much time we have to act. Many of the animals that live under the protection of darkness are on the verge of extinction and with them their invaluable services: pollinating insects, pest-hunting bats. Meanwhile, we humans have ever-worsening sleep, and plants are ageing prematurely.

Poets, philosophers, writers and artists draw inspiration from the dark. In the absence of external images, we create our own internally, with the help of our imagination. In the theatre, people talk about the black box, a portable stage room that is painted black where the actors can draw on their creative powers without any other distracting impressions. Another type of more laid back black box is established when we light candles in the autumn darkness and sit around the campfire in the summer evening. The Advent candleholders and the string lights in December create moods rather than recreating daylight. It's muted light we're seeking, the cosy lighting that promotes the relaxing darkness and intimate conversation.

I'm writing the last paragraph of this book during Earth Hour, on a piece of paper, in the glow of candles. Earth Hour, the World Wildlife Fund's worldwide climate protest, kicks off at the end of March each year, and was initially a call to make us aware of our energy waste. Now it can also be seen as a symbol of the fight against light pollution. In Berlin's parks, the effect of Earth Hour is totally measurable; the city's light pollution decreases during the darkened hour, although far from everyone participates in the event. At home, we pick out board games, put out freshly baked muffins, and make this recurring hour into a family tradition. But why stop at once a year? The lights don't always have to be on; there is more to be found in the dark than we think. It's fascinating to experience how our eyes slowly acclimatise and switch over to night vision, how the stars light up as the streetlights turn off, and how our conversations deepen when we lean back and rest our eyes.

The night is quite simply our friend – we rest in darkness, in its stillness and subtle beauty. We draw inspiration from the night, beyond the Milky Way and the distant lights. There's still life in the darkness of night, so let us take back the night, let us seize it.

Carpe noctem.

THE DARKNESS MANIFESTO

- Become aware of the darkness. The circadian rhythm is ancient and a precondition of all life, but the darkness of the night is currently kept at bay. Help to counter that.

- Protect the darkness. We are living in a world that seems to be awash with artificial light, but darkness is closer than you might think – merely a train trip, a walk or a turned-off phone away. Where do you find your darkness?

- Preserve the darkness in your surroundings. Turn off the lights when you leave a room and let your garden rest in darkness at night. Observe how the darkness and the shadows' nuances appear.

- Follow your inner rhythm. Let the darkness envelop you before you go to sleep, avoid blue light at night and let the sun reset the day in the morning.

- Discover nocturnal life. Take a journey beyond the city's dazzling skies and allow your eyes to adjust to the darkness. Watch the animals come out from their hiding places, their eyes glitter and their silhouettes pass by. Smell how the plants' scents change, hear how the new sounds take over.

- Seek out darkness. Observe the different phases of twilight and how the sun gives way to the moon and the stars. If you can, take yourself into the dark nights of midwinter and the mythical northern lights – a dazzling spectacle!

- Learn more about the darkness and its importance for the survival of animals and plants. Let yourself be inspired by literature and art from the time before the LED took over the night.

- Talk about darkness with the people around you – the more we spread knowledge about the benefits of darkness, the greater the chance that we can counteract problems caused by an excessively illuminated world.

- Influence your environment and be a role model in the fight against light pollution. Inform your municipality of which streetlights spread unnecessary amounts of light and how floodlighting can actually break environmental impact regulations. Participate in Earth Hour with your neighbours.

- Seize darkness. Become its friend and enjoy it – it will enrich your life.

ACKNOWLEDGEMENTS

Someone once said that writing isn't an occupation, it's a form of self-harm. But it's not as solitary an occupation as legend would have it. Many people have helped me along the way, through the corridors of darkness, with their knowledge, insights, advice and questions.

To get ideas and insight, facts, critiques and viewpoints from every angle on the subjects of darkness and light I talked to a variety of people before sitting down to write and throughout the writing process itself. Some people I met over coffee, others I just talked to on the phone, through a computer screen or by email. Many of the conversations have become important passages in the book, others have inspired what can be read between the lines. But all my meetings were equally important in the creation of this book. Everyone has contributed their thoughts on darkness and the necessity of darkness; their insights have been my companions throughout my work. And so I would like to humbly thank:

Andreas Nordin (cultural scientist), Anna Bergholtz (journalist), Anette Nääs (actor), Brett Seymoure (lepidopterist), Calle Bergil (biologist), Cecilia Wide (medical doctor, journalist and naturalist), Charlotta Thodelius (criminologist), Freja Holmberg (museum pedagogue), Frida Rångtell (sleep researcher), Frida Sandström (art writer), Helen Arfvidsson (curator, Museum of

World Culture), Henrik Aronsson (plant physiologist), Jarl Nordbladh (archaeologist), Jenny Lindström (zoophysiologist), Kajsa Sperling (lighting designer), Katja Lindblom (curator, Slottsskogen Observatory), Magnus Gelang (curator, Gothenburg Natural History Museum), Mattias Sandberg (cultural geographer), Micael Björk (sociologist), Mikael Cremle (water conservation officer), Serena Sabatini (archaeologist), Susanna Radovic (philosopher), Taylor Stone (technology philosopher), Åsa Gunnarsdotter (psychologist).

Enormous thanks to the team that published the book originally in Sweden, Lena Forssén (publisher) and Nils Sundberg (editor), who tirelessly cut, edited and polished the wording, as well as to those of you who read and proofread the book: Claes Bernes (astronomer), Emil V. Nilsson (botanist), Kennet Lundin (marine biologist) and Jenny Eklöf (biologist and medical doctor). For the English-language edition of the book, I'd like to thank my agents, Paul Sebes and Rik Kleuver, who got the book into the hands of editors Stuart William at Penguin Random House in the UK and Emily Polson and Colin Harrison at Simon & Schuster (Scribner) in the United States, and Elizabeth DeNoma who translated the book into English.

Finally, special thanks to Jens Rydell (1953–2021) (zoologist and nature photographer), with whom I've been experiencing and discussing bats and darkness since the late 1990s. I'll miss his company and counsel more than I can say. Without those adventures and conversations, this book would never have been written.

RESOURCES FOR FURTHER READING AND LISTENING

Bogard, P. 2013. *The End of Night: searching for natural darkness in an age of artificial light*. Fourth Estate.

Dark Sky Association: www.darksky.org.

Drake, N. 2019. Our nights are getting brighter, and earth is paying the price. *National Geographic*, 3 April.

Flash Forward, podcast. 2020. *Goodnight night*, 28 April.

Francis-Baker, T. 2019. *Dark Skies: a journey into the wild night*. Bloomsbury Wildlife.

Rich, C. & Longcore, T. (eds.). 2006. *Ecological Consequences of Artificial Night Lighting*. Island Press.

SOURCES

ALAN – International Conference on Artificial Light at Night. 2014–2018. *Abstract Booklets.*

Andersson, S. and others. 1998. Light, predation and the lekking behaviour of the ghost swift *Hepialus humuli* (L.) (Lepidoptera, Hepialidae). *Proceedings of the Royal Society of London B 265:1403.*

Angier, N. 1995. Modern life suppresses an ancient body rhythm. *New York Times*, 14 March.

Barnes, E. J. 1998. *The early career of George John Romanes, 1867–1878.* Undergraduate thesis. Newnham College, University of Cambridge.

BBC. 2016. *Planet Earth II.*

BBC. 2017. The making of Charles Messier's famous astronomy catalogue. *Sky at Night Magazine*, 3 August.

BBC. 2013. *The Secret Life of the Cat.*

Bennie, J. and others. 2015. Cascading effects of artificial light at night: resource-mediated control of herbivores in a grassland ecosystem. *Philosophical Transactions of the Royal Society B 370:1667.*

Bennie, J. and others. 2016. Ecological effects of artificial light at night on wild plants. *Journal of Ecology 104.*

Bentley, M. G. and others. 1999. Sexual satellites, moonlight and the nuptial dances of worms: the influence of the moon on the reproduction of marine animals. *Earth, Moon, and Planets 85.*

Bettini, A. 2017. *A Course in Classical Physics 4 – Waves and Light*. Springer International Publishing.

Bible, King James Version.

Bird, S. & Parker, J. 2014. Low levels of light pollution may block the ability of male glow-worms *(Lampyris noctiluca* L.) to locate females. *Journal of Insect Conservation 18:4.*

Björn, L. O. 2015. *Photobiology: the science of light and life*. Springer Science.

Bogard, P. 2013. *The End of Night: searching for natural darkness in an age of artificial light*. Fourth Estate.

Bortle, J. 2001. Introducing the Bortle Dark-Sky Scale. *Sky & Telescope*, February.

Broberg, G. 2016. *Nattens Historia: Nordiskt mörker och ljus under tusen år*. Natur & Kultur.

Brouwers, L. 2012. Animal vision evolved 700 million years ago. *Scientific American*, 20 November.

Brüning, A. and others. 2018. Influence of artificially induced light pollution on the hormone system of two common fish species, perch and roach, in a rural habitat. *Conservation Physiology 6:1*.

Campion, N. & Impey, C. (eds.). 2018. *Imagining Other Worlds: explorations in astronomy and culture*. Sophia Centre Press.

Carrington, D. 2019. Plummeting insect numbers 'threaten collapse of nature'. *Guardian*, 10 February.

Carson, R. 1962. *Silent Spring*. Houghton Mifflin.

Castellani, C. and others. 2012. Exceptionally well-preserved isolated eyes from Cambrian "Orsten" fossil assemblages of Sweden. *Palaeontology 55:3*.

Chepesiuk, R. 2009. Missing the Dark: Health Effects of Light Pollution. *Environmental Health Perspectives 117:1*.

Ciach, M. & Fröhlich, A. 2019. Ungulates in the City: light pollution and open habitats predict the probability of roe deer occurring in an urban environment. *Urban Ecosystems 22*.

Cuff, M. 2020. Lights out? Habitat loss and light pollution pose grave threat to UK glow worms. *i*, 4 February.

Dagens Nyheter. 2017. Ovanligt mörker över Stockholm oroade många. 17 October.

Danielsson, U. 2015. *Mörkret vid tidens ände. En bok om universums mörka sida*. Fri Tanke förlag.

Dark Sky Association: www.darksky.org.

Darwin, C. 1872. *The expression of the emotions in man and animals*. Fontana Press.

Dauchy, R. T. and others. 2014. Circadian and melatonin disruption by exposure to light at night drives intrinsic resistance to tamoxifen therapy in breast cancer. *Cancer Research 74:15*.

Depledge, M. and others. 2010. Light pollution in the sea. *Marine Pollution Bulletin 60*.

Desouhant, E. and others. 2018. Mechanistic, ecological, and evolutionary consequences of artificial light at night for insects: review and prospective. *Entomologia Experimentalis et Applicata 167*.

Di Domenico, A. 2019. European Union Adopts New Guidance to Reduce Light Pollution. *Environmental protection*, 6 December.

Dimovski, A. M. & Robert, K. A. 2018. Artificial light pollution: Shifting spectral wavelengths to mitigate physiological and health consequences in a nocturnal marsupial mammal. *Journal of Experimental Zoology Part A: Ecological and Integrative Physiology 329:8–9*.

Doctor, R. M. and others. 2008. *The Encyclopedia of Phobias, Fears, and Anxieties*. Facts on File.

Dokken, P. 2019. Varför är mörkret viktigt, Kajsa Sperling? *Göteborgs-Posten*, 23 March.

Dominoni, D. M. and others. 2013. Clocks for the city: circadian differences between forest and city songbirds. *Proceedings of the Royal Society of London B 280:1763*.

Drake, N. 2019. Our nights are getting brighter, and earth is paying the price. *National Geographic*, 3 April.

Duarte, C. and others. 2019. Artificial light pollution at night (ALAN) disrupts the distribution and circadian rhythm of a sandy beach isopod. *Environmental Pollution 248*.

Edqvist, B. & Eklöf, J. 2018. *Fladdermusen – i en mytisk värld*. Bokpro.

Ekirch, A. R. 2005. *At Day's Close: Night in Times Past*. W. W. Norton & Co.

Eklöf, J. 2008. *Djurens evolution*. Caracal Publishing.

Eklöf, J. & Rydell, J. 2015. *Fladdermöss – i en värld av ekon*. Hirschfeld förlag.

Eklöf, J. & Rydell, J. 2018. Det dödliga ljuset. *Forskning & Framsteg*, 27 September.

Eliasson, C. 2020. *Växter reagerar på ljus inom bråkdelen av en sekund*. Press release. University of Gothenburg, 31 March.

Elgert, C. and others. 2020. Reproduction under light pollution: maladaptive response to spatial variation in artificial light in a glow-worm. *Proceedings of the Royal Society of London B 287:1931*.

Emlen, S. T. 1975. The stellar-orientation system of a migratory bird. *Scientific American 233:2*.

Englund, P. 1991. *Förflutenhetens landskap*. Atlantis.

Entomologischer Verein Krefeld: www.entomologica.org.

European Festival of the Night: www.nightfestival.se.

Falchi, F. and others. 2016. The new world atlas of artificial night sky brightness. *Science Advances 2:6.*

Falchi, F. and others. 2019. Light pollution in USA and Europe: the good, the bad and the ugly. *Journal of Environmental Management 248.*

Farnworth, B. and others. 2018. Photons and foraging: artificial light at night generates avoidance behaviour in male, but not female, New Zealand weta. *Environmental Pollution 236.*

Farrington, D. P. & Welsh, B. C. 2007. *Förbättrad utomhusbelysning och brottsprevention: en systematisk forskningsgenomgång.* Brå. Rapport 2007:28.

Fimmerstad, L. (s.a.). Elljuset tränger undan gaslyktorna i Stockholm. stockholmshistoria.com.

Firebaugh, A. & Haynes, K. J. 2019. Light pollution may create demographic traps for nocturnal insects. *Basic and Applied Ecology 34.*

FISHBIO. 2018. Some like it dark: light pollution and salmon survival, 4 June.

Flash Forward, podcast. 2020. *Goodnight night*, 28 April.

Fobert, E. K. and others. 2019. Artificial light at night causes reproductive failure in clownfish. *Biology Letters 15:7.*

Folkminnesuppteckning, Broby, Lund 1874. DAL 1874:32.

Foster, J. J. and others. 2019. Orienting to polarized light at night – matching lunar skylight to performance in a nocturnal beetle. *Journal of Experimental Biology 222.*

Fox, D. 2016. What sparked the Cambrian explosion? *Nature 530:18.*

Francis-Baker, T. 2019. *Dark Skies: a journey into the wild night.* Bloomsbury Wildlife.

Fredelius, A. 2016. Rätt ljus ger piggare läkare. *Ny Teknik*, 20 June.

Gallaway, T. and others. 2010. The economics of global light pollution. *Ecological Economics 69:3.*

Garcia-Saenz, A. and others. 2018. Evaluating the association between artificial light-at-night exposure and breast and prostate cancer risk in Spain (MCC-Spain Study). *Environmental Health Perspectives 126:4.*

Gardner, J. 2018. Fladdermöss hjälper ekologisk vinodling. *Vinjournalen*, 27 August.

Garnert, J. 2012. August Strindbergs ljus. *Ljuskultur 4:12.*

Garnert, J. 2016. *Ut ur mörkret. Ljusets och belysningens kulturhistoria.* Historiska media.

Gaston, K. J. 2012. Reducing the ecological consequences of night-time light pollution: options and developments. *Journal of Applied Ecology 49*.

Gaukel Andrews, C. 2018. The largest migration on earth is vertical. NatHab.com, 21 August.

Gauthreaux, S. A. & Belser, C. G. 2006. Effects of artificial night lighting on migrating birds. In: Rich, C. & Longcore, T. (eds.). *Ecological Consequences of Artificial Night Lighting*. Island Press.

Gibbens, S. 2018. See 'underwater snowstorm' of coral reproducing. *National Geographic*, 8 January.

Gibbens, S. 2020. As the Arctic warms, light pollution may pose a new threat to marine life. *National Geographic*, 5 March.

Griffith Observatory: www.griffithobservatory.org.

Grenis, K. & Murphy, S. M. 2018. Direct and indirect effects of light pollution on the performance of an herbivorous insect. *Insect Science 26:4*.

Grønne, J. 2019. Tusentals meteorer målar himlen. *Illustrerad Vetenskap*, 12 August.

Guilford, T. 2019. Light pollution causes object collisions during local nocturnal manoeuvring flight by adult Manx Shearwaters *Puffinus puffinus*. *Seabird 31*.

Gustafsson, B. (s.a.) Fjärilar insamlade i ljusfälla på Naturhistoriska riksmuseets tak. Manuscript. *Hagabladet*.

Hadenius, P. 2019. *Paus: Konsten att göra något annat*. Natur & Kultur.

Hadhazy, A. 2010. Fact or fiction: the days (and nights) are getting longer. *Scientific American*, 14 June.

Haim, A. & Zubidat, A. E. 2015. Artificial light at night: melatonin as a mediator between the environment and epigenome. *Philosophical Transactions of the Royal Society of London. Series B, Biological Sciences 370:1667*.

Hallemar, D. 2017. *Disciplinerande ljus och förlåtande mörker*. OBS, Sveriges Radio P1, 20 February.

Hallmann, C. A. and others. 2017. More than 75 percent decline over 27 years in total flying insect biomass in protected areas. *PLoS ONE 12:10*.

Hansen, J. 2017. Night shift work and risk of breast cancer. *Current Environmental Health Report 4:3*.

Hart, A. 2018. The rise of astrotourism: why your next adventure should include star-gazing. *Telegraph*, 11 July.

Harvard Health Letter. 2012. *Blue light has a dark side*. Harvard Health Publishing, May.

Heinrich, B. 2014. *The Homing Instinct: Meaning & Mystery in Animal Migration*. Houghton Mifflin Harcourt.

Heintzenberg, F. 2013. *Nordiska nätter: djurliv mellan skymning och gryning*. Bio & Fokus Förlag.

Howard, J. 2019. These fish eggs aren't hatching. The culprit? Light pollution. *National Geographic*, 9 July.

Hughes, H. C. 1999. *Sensory Exotica: a world beyond human experience*. Bradford Books.

Hunt, R. 1849. *The Poetry of Science: or, studies of the physical phenomena of nature*. Reeve, Benham, and Reeve.

Härdig, A. 2019. Myter om månen. *Populär Astronomi 1*.

Hölker, F. and others. 2010. Light pollution as a biodiversity threat. *Trends in Ecology & Evolution 25:12*.

Hölker, F. and others. 2010. The dark side of light: a transdisciplinary research agenda for light pollution policy. *Ecology and Society 15:4*.

I mörkret med . . ., podcast: www.imorkretmed.se.

Interactive map of London's gas lamps: https://londonist.com/london/maps/an-interactive-map-of-london-s-gas-lamps.

International Dark Sky Association. 2012. *Fighting Light Pollution: smart lighting solutions for individuals and communities*. Stackpole Books.

Irenius, L. 2019. Gläds åt mörkret – det är hotat. *Svenska Dagbladet*, 19 November.

Jabr, F. 2017. How moonlight sets nature's rhythms. *Smithsonian Magazine*, 21 June.

Jechow, A. 2019. Observing the impact of WWF Earth Hour on urban light pollution: a case study in Berlin 2018 using differential photometry. *Sustainability 11:3*.

Jechow, A. & Hölker, F. 2019. Snowglow – The amplification of skyglow by snow and clouds can exceed full moon illuminance in suburban areas. *Journal of Imaging 5:69*.

Johannisson, K. 2009. *Melankoliska rum*. Albert Bonniers Förlag.

Jones, L. and others. 2005. *Encyclopedia of Religion*. Macmillan Reference.

Josefsson, L. 2019. Elegi över ett spinneri. *Göteborgs-Posten*, 10 October.

Jägerbrand, A. K. 2018. *LED-belysningens effekter på djur och natur med rekommendationer: Fokus på nordiska förhållanden och känsliga arter och grupper*. Calluna AB.

Jönköpings Läns Museum. 2019. Konstverket SAMTAL.

Kachi Lodge, Bolivia: www.kachilodge.com.

Kafka, F. 2014 (reprint). *Man hör varandra bättre i mörker: brev 1918–juni 1920*. Bakhåll.

Karlsson, B-L. and others. 2002. No lunar phobia in swarming insectivorous bats (family Vespertilionidae). *Journal of Zoology 256:4*.

Kay, J. 2014. Nighttime lights reset birds' internal clocks, threatening dawn's chorus. *National Geographic*, 6 September.

Klarsfeld, A. 2013. At the dawn of chronobiology. *Bibnum*.

Knop, E. and others. 2017. Artificial light at night as a new threat to pollination. *Nature 548: 7666*.

Konstform, podcast. Episode 14: Mörker.

Kronberg, K. and others. 2018. *Minnet av Narva: om troféer, propaganda och historiebruk*. Nordic Academic Press.

Krönström, J. 2009. *Control of Bioluminescence: operating the light switch in photophores from marine animals*. PhD thesis. Department of Zoology, University of Gothenburg.

Kunz, T. and others. 2011. Ecosystem services provided by bats. *Annals of the New York Academy of Sciences 1223*.

Land, M. F. & Nilsson, D-E. 2002. *Animal Eyes*. Oxford University Press.

Last, K. S. and others. 2016. Moonlight drives ocean-scale mass vertical migration of zooplankton during the arctic winter. *Current Biology 26*.

Lawal, S. 2020. Fireflies have a mating problem: the lights are always on. *New York Times*, 3 February.

Leanderson, P. 2018. *Ljusföroreningar och mörkret som försvann*. Arbets- och miljömedicinbloggen, 30 August.

Light Pollution Map: www.lightpollutionmap.info.

Liljemalm, A. 2016. Utrotningshotat nattmörker. *Forskning & Framsteg*, 15 March.

Longcore, T. & Rich, C. 2004. Ecological light pollution. *Frontiers in Ecology and the Environment 2:4*.

Luftfartsstyrelsens författningssamling. 2007. LFS 2007:50, Serie OPS. Utgivare: Byström Möller L.

Lundqvist, Å. 1990. Krönika. *Dagens Nyheter*, 21 December.

Lövemyr, A. 2018. *Att skapa plats för mörker och natthimlen: belysning och människan i stadens nattlandskap*. SLU, Fakulteten för landskapsarkitektur, trädgårds-och växtproduktionsvetenskap.

Macgregor, C. J. and others. 2015. Pollination by nocturnal Lepidoptera, and the effects of light pollution: a review. *Ecological Entomology 40*.

Macgregor, C. J. and others. 2019. Effects of street lighting technologies on the success and quality of pollination in a nocturnally pollinated plant. *Ecosphere 10:1.*

Macgregor, C. J. and others. 2019. Moth biomass increases and decreases over 50 years in Britain. *Nature Ecology and Evolution 3.*

Manríquez, P. H. and others. 2019. Artificial light pollution influences behavioral and physiological traits in a keystone predator species, *Concholepas concholepas. Science of the Total Environment 661.*

Marsh, G. P. 1864. *Man and Nature: or, physical geography as modified by human action.* Charles Scribner.

Martini, S. & Haddock, S. 2017. Quantification of bioluminescence from the surface to the deep sea demonstrates its predominance as an ecological trait. *Scientific Reports 7.*

Martinson, H. 1953. *Cikada,* Albert Bonniers Förlag.

McCarthy, D. D. & Seidelmann, K. P. 2018. *Time: from earth rotation to atomic physics.* Cambridge University Press.

McConnell, A. and others. 2010. Effect of artificial light on marine invertebrate and fish abundance in an area of salmon farming. *Marine Ecology Progress Series 419.*

McGrane, S. 2017. The German amateurs who discovered insect armageddon. *New York Times,* 4 December.

McMenamin, M. A. S. 1998. *The Garden of Ediacara.* Columbia University Press.

Meravi, N. & Prajapati, S. K. 2020. Effect street light pollution on the photosynthetic efficiency of different plants. *Biological Rhythm Research 51.*

Merritt, D. J. & Clarke, A. 2012. The impact of cave lighting on the bioluminescent display of the Tasmanian glow-worm *Arachnocampa tasmaniensis. Journal of Insect Conservation 17:1.*

Milosevic, I. & McCabe, R. E. 2015. *The Psychology of Irrational Fear.* Greenwood.

Moore, M. V. and others. 2000. Urban light pollution alters the diel vertical migration of *Daphnia. SIL Proceedings 27.*

Morris, H. 2017. The casino light beam that's so bright it has its own ecosystem (and pilots use it to navigate). *Telegraph,* 24 August.

Murakami, H. 2011. *1Q84.* Doubleday.

Musila, S. and others. 2019. No lunar phobia in insectivorous bats in Kenya. *Mammalian Biology 95.*

Mårtenson, J. & Turander, R. 2007. *Kungliga Djurgården*. Wahlström & Widstrand.

Nagel, T. 1974. What is it like to be a bat? *The Philosophical Review 83:4*.

Netflix. 2020. *Night on Earth*.

Nichols, C. A. & Alexander, K. 2018. Creeping in the night: What might ecologists be missing? *PLoS ONE 13:6*.

Nilsson, D-E. 2012. Havsmonstrets vakande öga. *Forskning & Framsteg*, 7 August.

Nobel Prize in Physics press release. 2014.

Nobel Prize in Physics press release. 2019.

Nobel Prize in Physiology or Medicine press release. 2017.

Noche Zero: https://lightcollective.net/light/ing/noche_zero.

Nordstrand, M. 2009. Stökigt med fullmåne. *Örnsköldsviks Allehanda*, 7 August.

Nygren, A. and others. 2017. Nationalnyckeln till Sveriges flora och fauna. Ringmaskar: Havsborstmaskar, Annelida: Polychaeta: Aciculata. SLU ArtDatabanken.

Nyström, J. 2018. Koralldöden har blivit fem gånger värre. *Forskning & Framsteg*, 4 January.

Oliveira, A. G. and others. 2015. Circadian control sheds light on fungal bioluminescence. *Current Biology 25*.

Owens, A. C. S. and others. 2020. Light pollution is a driver of insect declines. *Biological Conservation 241* (pre-published online, November 2019).

Pape Møller, A. 2019. Parallel declines in abundance of insects and insectivorous birds in Denmark over 22 years. *Ecology and Evolution 9:11*.

Perry, G. and others. 2008. Effects of night lights on urban reptiles and amphibians. *Herpetological Conservation 3*.

Pettit, H. (& Agence France-Presse). 2017. Elephants threatened by poachers are evolving to become nocturnal so they can travel safely at night. *Daily Mail*, 13 September.

Pinzon-Rodriguez, A. and others. 2018. Expression patterns of cryptochrome genes in avian retina suggest involvement of Cry4 in light-dependent magnetoreception. *Journal of the Royal Society 15:140*.

Pixar. 2003. *Finding Nemo*.

Professor Magenta, podcast. Episodes 7–9, Mörkertrilogin.

Pulgar, J. and others. 2019. Endogenous cycles, activity patterns and energy expenditure of an intertidal fish is modified by artificial light pollution at night (ALAN). *Environmental Pollution 244*.

Raap, T. and others. 2015. Light pollution disrupts sleep in free-living animals. *Scientific Reports 5: 13557.*

Restaurang Svartklubben: http://svartklubben.com.

Riccucci, M. & Rydell, J. 2017. Bats in the Florentine Renaissance: from darkness to enlightenment (Chiroptera). *Lynx 48.*

Riccucci, M. 2008. Lazzaro Spallanzani. *Bat Research News 49:4.*

Rich, C. & Longcore, T. (eds.). 2006. *Ecological Consequences of Artificial Night Lighting.* Island Press.

Romanes, G. R. 1883. *Mental Evolution in Animals: with a posthumous essay on instinct by Charles Darwin.* Cambridge University Press.

Russ, A. and others. 2015. Seize the night: European blackbirds (*Turdus merula*) extend their foraging activity under artificial illumination. *Journal of Ornithology 156.*

Rybnikova, N. & Portnov, B. A. 2018. Population-level study links short-wavelength nighttime illumination with breast cancer incidence in a major metropolitan area. *Chronobiology International 35:9.*

Rydell, J. and others. 2020. Dramatic decline of northern bat *Eptesicus nilssonii* in Sweden over 30 years. *Royal Society Open Science 7:2.*

Rydell, J. and others. 2017. Age of enlightenment: long-term effects of outdoor aesthetic lights on bats in churches. *Royal Society Open Science 4:8.*

Rångtell, F. 2019. *If only I could sleep, maybe I could remember.* PhD thesis. Department of Neuroscience, Uppsala University.

Salleh, A. 2015. Light pollution delays wallaby reproduction and puts joeys at risk. *ABC News*, 30 September.

Sánchez-Bayo, F. & Wyckhuys, K. A. G. 2019. Worldwide decline of the entomofauna: a review of its drivers. *Biological Conservation 232.*

Sandberg, S. 2019. *Mørke – stjerner, redsel og fem netter på Finse.* Samlaget.

Santos, C. D. 2010. Effects of artificial illumination on the nocturnal foraging of waders. *Acta Oecologica 36:2.*

Saving Nemo Conservation Fund: www.savingnemo.org.

Scharping, N. 2018. Why China's artificial moon probably won't work. *Astronomy*, 26 October.

Schoppert, S. 2017. *Emerging from the darkness: 9 creation myths from different cultures. History Collection*, 11 April.

Segedin, K. 2016. Every turtle featured in harrowing *Planet Earth II* segment was saved. BBC Earth.

Sempler, K. 2009. Den märkliga manicken från Antikythera. *Ny Teknik*, 3 March.

Sempler, K. 2018. När Stockholm fick elektriskt ljus. *Ny Teknik*, 4 February.

Singhal, R. K. and others. 2019. Eco-physiological responses of artificial night light pollution in plants. *Russian Journal of Plant Physiology 66*.

Škvareninová, J. and others. 2017. Effects of light pollution on tree phenology in the urban environment. *Moravian Geographical Reports 25:4*.

SMHI Kunskapsbanken: https://www.smhi.se/kunskapsbanken.

Smith, M. 2009. Time to turn off the lights. *Nature 457:27*.

Söderström, B. 2016. *Hur tänker din katt?* Bonnier Fakta.

Solly, M. 2019. Swarms of Grasshoppers Invading Las Vegas Are Visible on Radar. *Smithsonian Magazine*, 30 July.

Sperling, N. 1991. The disappearance of darkness. In: Crawford, D. L. (ed.). *Light pollution, Radio Interference, and Space Debris*, volume 17. Astronomical Society of the Pacific Conference Series.

Squires, W. A. & Hanson, H. E. 1918. The destruction of birds at the lighthouses on the coast of California. *The Condor 20:1*.

Stagnelius, E. J. c.1820. Vän! I förödelsens stund. (Electronic resource).

Steinbach, R. 2015. The effect of reduced street lighting on road casualties and crime in England and Wales: controlled interrupted time series analysis. *Journal of Epidemiology & Community Health 69:11*.

Stevens, R. G. 2016. What rising light pollution means for our health. BBC Future.

Stone, T. 2017. Light Pollution: A case study in framing an environmental problem. *Ethics, Policy & Environment 20:3*.

Stone, T. 2018. The Value of Darkness: A Moral Framework for Urban Nighttime Lighting. *Science Engineering Ethics 24*.

Strindberg, A. 1884. *Om det allmänna missnöjet, dess orsaker och botemedel*. Albert Bonniers Förlag.

Strömdahl, H. 2015. Candela – grundenheten för grundstorheten ljusstyrka. *Kemivärlden Biotech med Kemisk Tidskrift 2*.

Svensson, A. M. & Rydell, J. 1998. Mercury vapour lamps interfere with the bat defence of tympanate moths (*Operophtera* spp.; Geometridae). *Animal Behaviour 55:1*.

Svensson, A. M. and others. 2002. Avoidance of bats by water striders (*Aquarius najas*, Hemiptera). *Hydrobiologia 489*.

Svensson, P. 2019. *Ålevangeliet: berättelsen om världens mest gåtfulla fisk*. Albert Bonniers Förlag.

Sveriges Radio P1. 2015. Vem äger mörkret? *Vetenskapsradion Klotet*, 19 August.

Sveriges Radio P1. 2017. Så påverkas naturen av allt mer ljus. *Naturmorgon,* 30 December.

Sveriges Radio P1. 2019. Fysikpristagaren Peebles tog fram universums recept. *Vetandets värld,* 5 December.

Sveriges Radio P1. 2019. Utflykter i natten – och älgar som far illa av varma somrar. *Naturmorgon,* 30 November.

Sveriges Radio P4 Sjuhärad. 2018. *Ljuset är nästa miljökatastrof,* 9 January.

SVT Nyheter. 2011. Mångalen? – Inte så galet, 11 November.

SVT Nyheter. 2019. Upplysta städer knäcker nattdjur, 7 July.

Tanizaki, J. 2001. *In Praise of Shadows.* Vintage Classics.

The Nobel Prize Nomination Database: www.nobelprize.org/nomination/redirector/?redir=archive.

Tidskriften Pilgrim 9. 2009.

Touzot, M. and others. 2019. Artificial light at night disturbs the activity and energy allocation of the common toad during the breeding period. *Conservation Physiology 7:1.*

Tracy Aviary: https://tracyaviary.org.

Tycho Brahe-museet: www.landskrona.se/se-gora/kultur-noje/museero-chkonsthall/tycho-brahe-museet.

Tähkämö, L. and others. 2018. Systematic review of light exposure impact on human circadian rhythm. *Chronobiology International 36:2.*

Van Doren, B. M. and others. High-intensity urban light installation dramatically alters nocturnal bird migration. *Proceedings of the National Academy of Sciences 114.*

Van Geffen, K. G. and others. 2015. Artificial night lighting disrupts sex pheromone in a noctuid moth. *Ecological Entomology 40.*

Van Langevelde, F. and others. 2018. Declines in moth populations stress the need for conserving dark nights. *Global Change Biology 24:3.*

Vogel, G. 2017. Where have all the insects gone? *Science*, 10 May.

Voigt, C. C. and others. 2018: Guidelines for consideration of bats in lighting projects. EUROBATS *8.*

Wallace, D. R. 2004. *Beasts of Eden: walking whales, dawn horses, and other enigmas of mammal evolution.* University of California Press.

Westerdahl, C. 1982. Kulturhistoria och grottor. *Svenska grottor 5.*

Wheeling, K. 2015. Artificial light may alter underwater ecosystems. *Science,* 28 April.

Whyte, C. 2019. Light pollution's effects on birds may help to spread West Nile virus. *New Scientist*, 24 July.

Winger, B. M. and others. 2019. Nocturnal flight-calling behaviour predicts vulnerability to artificial light in migratory birds. *Proceedings of the Royal Society of London B 286:1900.*

Wistrand, S. 2015. Eugène Jansson – inte bara blåmålare. *Kulturdelen*, 26 June.

Witherington, B. E. and others. 2014 (revised 3rd edition). *Understanding, Assessing, and Resolving Light-Pollution Problems on Sea Turtle Nesting Beaches.* Florida Fish and Wildlife Conservation Commission, Technical Reports.

Wright Jr, K. P. and others. 2013. Entrainment of the human circadian clock to the natural light-dark cycle. *Current Biology 23.*

Zachos, E. 2016. Too much light at night causes spring to come early. *National Geographic*, 28 June.

Zdanowicz, C. 2019. Hordes of grasshoppers have invaded Las Vegas. CNN, 27 July.

Zhang, Z. 2020. Man-made moon to shed light on Chengdu in 2020. *China Daily*, 19 October.

Zubidat, A. E. & Haim, A. 2017. Artificial light at night – a novel lifestyle risk factor for metabolic disorder and cancer morbidity. *Journal of Basic and Clinical Physiology and Pharmacology 28:4.*

INDEX

Abisko National Park, Sweden 184
Africa 21, 25, 43, 53, 74, 111, 220
agriculture 3, 22, 60, 186
Akasaki, Isamu 179
algae 9, 43, 89, 90, 95, 99, 101, 103, 105
Amano, Hiroshi 179
amateur astronomical twilight 128
Andersdotter, Stina 39
Andes 177, 183
Andromeda Galaxy 152
Animal Behaviour 57
Anthropocene 4, 16, 17–18
antidepressants 165
Antikythera Mechanism 144
anxiety 144
aphids 83–4
apple tree 82
Arctic Circle 148, 150, 159
Arctic tern 71
Arcturus 127
Aristotle 44, 153
artists, night and 152–3
astronomical twilight 128, 143
Astro-tourism 183–4
Atacama Desert, Chile 177–8
Athena 45
Auroral Oval 149–50
autumn 27, 46, 66–7, 68, 74, 81, 82, 89, 127, 141, 143, 155, 174, 201
autumn equinox 127
barbastelle bat 113
bats
- age of 116
- China and 173–4
- churches and 1–3, 115–18
- Covid-19 and 119
- droppings/guano 1, 121
- echolocation 43–4, 45–9, 56–7
- ecosystem services and 122
- eyesight 43–4
- insect predation 118–21
- malaria and 120–1
- mating 68
- megabats 43–4
- Michelangelo's sculptures of 173
- moon and 143
- moths and 14, 55, 60, 113
- New Zealand and 111–12
- nightjar and 47
- pest control 119–22
- pollinators 53, 120
- rice growing and 119–20
- Skansen and 190–1
- threat to 115–22
- twilight and 1–3, 15, 51–4
- 'What is it like to be a bat?' (Nagel) 12–13
- winegrowers and 121–2
- *See also individual species name*

beech tree 82
bees 9, 13, 25, 31, 120

Berlin, Germany 159, 201
Besson, Luc 105
Betelgeuse 73
Bible 21, 172–3
Biblioteca Medicea Laurenziana, Florence 173
big bang 37, 131, 132, 133
Big Blue, The (film) 105
bioluminescence 12, 89–90, 91, 92, 106
birds
  confused by light 65–9, 71–5, 77–9
  declines in population numbers 65–9, 71–5
  eyesight 42
  insects and 29–30, 56, 65
  migration 65–9, 71–5, 77–9
  song 4, 11, 65–9
  See also individual species name
bird's-foot trefoil 83
blackbird, European 65–7
Blanch's Café, Stockholm 154
blue light 71, 89, 126, 150, 161, 163, 165, 166, 167, 203
blue moment 150
Bogard, Paul: *The End of Night: Searching for Natural Darkness in an Age of Artificial Light* 137–8
Bohuslän, Sweden 89
Bollebygd, Sweden 147, 199
Bortle, John E. 136
Bortle scale 136–8, 185
Brahe, Tycho 128
breast cancer 166
bristle worms 103–4, 105, 108
brown-long-eared bat 1, 113, 115–16, 191
Brunkeberg Square, Stockholm 137
bush crickets (*Tettigoniidae*) 111
butterfly fish 98, 118
butterfly orchid 9, 13

cabbage moth 26–7
cabbage thistle 87
cacti 53, 183
Cambrian explosion 37–40, 43, 155
camouflage 59, 113
Campbell, John 128
Canary Islands 184
cancer 18, 92, 98, 100, 166
Capella 127
capriole 13
carbon dioxide emissions 16–17, 122
car park 4, 15, 26, 117, 147, 199
Carson, Rachel: *Silent Spring* 65
Cassini, Giovanni Domenico 146
cats 45, 52–3, 112
Charles X Gustav, King of Sweden 185
Charles XII, King of Sweden 137, 200
cheetah 53
Chengdu, China 145
China 38, 145, 173–4
China Daily 145
chlorophyll 81
circadian rhythm 3, 4, 7–10, 32, 33, 71, 73, 91, 107, 113, 161, 199, 203
cities 3, 4, 15–16, 17, 21, 65–7, 77–9, 82, 93–4, 121, 129, 138, 146, 147, 150, 151–4, 157, 158, 159–60, 175–7, 180, 184, 187, 191, 201. *See also individual city name*
city parks 189–90
civil twilight 127–8, 163
Clement VII, Pope 173
climate change 3, 22, 82, 86, 100, 103, 201
cloud 57, 58, 66, 72, 74, 85, 126, 127, 147, 160
clownfish 97–100, 102
cnidarians 101, 108
cockchafer 14, 15
collembola 108
colour
  animal colour/pattern/camouflage, light pollution and 59–63
  coral and 99, 100, 101

eye and 41–3
plants and 81–3
twilight and 126–7
Columbus, Christopher 183–4
comets 135, 139, 140–1, 146, 152
compass, inner 71, 74
C/1743 X1/Klinkenberg-Chéseaux comet 135
cones, retina 41–3, 146, 176
CONVERSATION (live art installation) 194–5
conversation, darkness and 193–7
copepods 89
coral reefs 4, 97–100, 101–4, 105, 108
cornea 41
Cornwall 83
cosmic background radiation 132
Crab Nebula (Messier object 1) (M1) 135
creation stories 132, 172–3
crickets 20, 55–6, 111
crustaceans 25, 40, 89, 106, 108
Crutzen, Paul 16
cryptochromes 71–2, 161
cyanobacteria 8–9
Cymorek, Siegfried 30–1

Dag ('Day') 172
damselflies 84
dark energy 132
dark matter 131–3
darkness
animals and *see individual animal species name*
conversation and 193–7
creation stories and 172–3
cycle of 7–10
dark energy 132
dark matter 131–3
dark park 185–7, 190
defenders of 157–8
defining 171–4
Daubenton's bat 191
Djurgården, Stockholm and 189–91, 199
experiences in 11–14
eyesight and *see* eyesight
light, relationship with 171–3
linguistics and 171–2
living darkness 175–6, 191
loneliness and 193
manifesto 203–4
night sky and 135–8
nyctophobia (fear of the dark) 17
plants and 81–7
security and 107, 173, 180, 186–7, 193, 200
speed of 132–3, 172
twilight and *see* twilight
tourism 183–7
dark park 185–7, 190
Dark Sky Community 185, 187
Darwin, Charles 19, 48, 75
day, length of 8
DDT 65
deer 68, 169
Denmark 184–5
depression 18, 153, 160, 165
Diana, goddess 92
dinoflagellates (single-celled algae) 43, 89, 91
dinosaur 30, 52
diode 4, 15, 61, 179–81
Djurgården, Stockholm 189–91, 199
Drese, Melanie 121
dung beetle 25–6
durian ('stinkfruit') 120
dusk 1, 10, 24, 42, 43, 51, 53, 61, 95, 99, 100, 112, 113, 115, 122, 126, 127, 159, 163, 191

Earth Hour 201, 204
earthquakes 91
Los Angeles (1994) 151
East Australian Current 97
echolocation 43–4, 45–9, 56
ecliptic 146

ecosystem services 122
Edison, Thomas Alva 154
eel 47, 95, 107, 141
eggs 24, 26, 27, 61, 67, 68, 93, 94–5, 97, 99, 100, 102, 111
Einstein, Albert 125, 131
Eisner, Minze 195
Eklöf (née Jonsson), Jenny Alfrida (great-grandmother of author) 115, 116, 156
Eklöf, Johan (great-grandfather of author) 115, 200, 206
electricity 75, 152–4, 155–8, 165, 195, 200
electromagnetic radiation 126, 132
elephant 53
El Niño 101–2
Emlen, Stephen T. 73–4
Enlightenment 157
Entomologischer Verein Krefeld (Krefeld Insect Society) 30, 31
equator 101, 127
Erik Hård af Segerstad 115
Eureka Valley, Death Valley National Park 138
evolution 19–20, 38, 43, 52, 54, 86, 111, 120
exhaustion 3, 24, 165
eye/eyesight
  acclimatisation to darkness 2–3, 7, 17, 176, 201, 203–4
  designing lighting adapted for 179–81
  first, evolution of 37–40
  human anatomy and 41–4 *see also individual component of eye*
  lighting design and 180–1
  navigation and 71–5
  nocturnal senses and 45–9
  ocean and 89–92
  twilight animals and 51–4

false dawn 146
fertiliser 121
Finding Nemo (film) 97–9
fireflies 63, 92
fish fry 98, 108
Flagstaff, Arizona, USA 187
Fledermaus 121
Flinders University, Adelaide 98, 99
France 121, 122, 135, 153, 185–6, 187
Francis, Pope 173
frogs 13, 55–6, 143
fruit bat 43–4

galaxies, rotation of 131
gametes 102
gamma radiation 126
Garden Island 68–9
gas lamps 153–4, 155, 157
Geminids 147–8
ghost moths 59–61
giant crab spiders 25–6
giant squid 90
Global Change Biology 31
glow-worms 61–3, 92
Gogh, Vincent van: *Starry Night* 152–3
Gondwanaland 111
Gothenburg, Sweden 56, 81, 107, 117, 147, 151–2, 160, 206
Goya, Francisco de 51
grasshopper 11, 21, 111, 112
Great Barrier Reef 97, 102
Great Belt of Denmark 185
Great Salt Lake, Utah 78
green lacewings 84
greenhouses 85–6
green sea turtle 94
Griffin, Donald 47–8
Griffith Observatory 151
Groningen, Netherlands 186
guano 1, 121
Gulf of Bothnia 148
Gustav III, King 189

Härnösand, Sweden 85
Halley's Comet 152

Hall, Jeffrey C. 7
Hansen, Johnni 166
Harvard University 47, 163
hearing 14, 43–4, 45–9, 56–7, 59, 108, 191–2, 195, 204
hedgehog 2–3, 45
Helsingborg 184
herring 108
hibernation 149, 161–2
Hoffmann, E. T. A.: 'The Sandman' 47
Homo, birth of genus 136
Honduras 105
honey fungus 12
Hong Kong 17
Hornborga, Lake 78
hormone systems 21, 33, 69, 161, 162, 166
hoverflies 84
Hunt, Robert 82–3
Huygens, Christiaan 125
hypothalamus 67

ice hotel, Jukkasjärvi 184
Iceland 19, 24, 184
India 74
indigo bunting 73
infrared light 126
insects
  collapse in population numbers 22, 29–33, 65
  navigation/drawn to light sources 20–2, 23–7, 29–33, 46
  numbers of species 23
  See also individual insect species name
International Dark-Sky Association (IDA) 186
International Union for Conservation of Nature: Red List of Threatened Species 94
In the dark with . . . (podcast) 197
Io 125
iris 41
Isaiah 173

Jansson, Eugène 153
Japan 63, 145, 175–7, 191, 193
jellyfish 89, 98
Jord ('Earth') 172
Jukkasjärvi 184
Jupiter 125, 138
Jurine, Charles 47

kaamos ('a constant darkness, a long, uninterrupted night') 148–50
Kachi Lodge, Bolivia 183–4
Kafka, Franz 195
Kakeled quarry, Kinnekulle Mountain 38–9
Karlstad Central Hospital 144, 167
killer whale 108
Korpilombolo, Pajala municipality, Norrbotten 148
Krau Wildlife Reserve, Malaysia 20
Kristina, Queen of Sweden 115

Ladulås, Magnus 189
ladybirds 84
Lagerstätte 40
lampposts 15, 56, 57, 175
lanterns 12, 59, 61, 74, 75, 108, 116, 137, 153, 161, 191, 193
La Paz, Bolivia 183
laws, light pollution 185–6, 187, 200
leafroller moths 121–2
leatherback turtle 94
LED (light-emitting diodes) 4, 83, 179–81, 204
Leipzig, Germany 66
Leonids 141
leptin 162, 166
life, origins of 8–9
light
  animals and *see individual animal species name*
  cities and *see* cities
  colour and *see* colour
  comets and *see* comets

light (*cont.*)
creation stories and 172–3
diode 179–81
dual nature of 125–6
electric 75, 152–4, 155–8, 165, 195, 200
eye/eyesight and *see* eye/eyesight
health problems and 165–7
industrial 155–8
intensity of 55, 83, 126, 167, 175, 176, 181
moon and *see* moon
navigation and *see* navigation
particles 125
plants and *see* plants
polar light/polar night 127, 147–50, 184
pollution *see* pollution, light
sea and 89–109
singing in the wrong 55–8
sleep and *see* sleep
speed of 125, 132–3, 172
sun and *see* sun
twilight *see* twilight
types of *see individual type name*
wave, as a 125, 126
wavelengths 33, 42, 48, 57, 59, 69, 82–3, 126, 167
wealth, as symbol of 200
light bulb 3, 15, 83, 154, 179
lighthouses 74, 178
lilac 13
Lindgren, Astrid 190
Liseberg amusement park, Gothenburg 117, 160
living darkness 175–6, 191
Logan 78
loggerhead turtle 94
Lomma 184
London 153–4, 157
loneliness 193
long-day growth 86
Long Point, Canada 74
Louis XV, King of France 135
Lucifer 92
Luciferin 92
lugworm 104
lunacy 144
Lundqvist, Åke 172
Lund University 116
Luxor Sky Beam, Las Vegas 20–1, 137

Madängsholm, Sweden 155
magnetic field 71–2, 149
magnetite 71
Magnus, Albertus 44; *De animalibus* ('On Animals') 44
Mairan, Jean-Jacque d'Ortous de 7
malaria 120–1
Malmberg, Sven 39
Måne (Moon) 172
manifesto, darkness 203–4
maple tree 81, 82
Mars 138, 183
Marsh, George Perkins: *Man and Nature: or, Physical Geography as Modified by Human Action* 16
Martinson, Harry 127, 175
mass die-off 29–33
mating
dance 14, 60, 63, 99, 143
impulse, distinguished 23–7
season 67, 68
song 55, 67
Mayol, Jacques 105
Meänkieli 148
Medici family 173–4
Medici, Lorenzo II de 174
melatonin 161–3, 165, 166
Menai Strait 108
menstruation 144
Mesoamerican Barrier Reef System 105
Messier, Charles 135–6, 137, 141
metabolism 162, 163
meteors 139, 140, 141, 146, 147

Michelangelo 173, 174
microwaves 126, 133
migrations 21, 32, 71–4, 77, 79, 95, 106–8
Milky Way 4, 136–7, 138, 151, 152, 164, 186, 201
Mimosa pudica 7, 9
Møller, Anders Pape 29–30
molluscs 89, 104, 106
Mön, Denmark 184–7
mongoose 53–4
moon
  artificial 145
  birth and 145
  lunacy and 145
  mating and 99, 102–4
  myths surrounding 145–6
  navigation and 3, 23–7
  ocean and 105–9
  sleep and 143–4
  twilight and *see* twilight
Mormons 78
mosquito 20, 61, 62, 118, 119, 120
Mossebo Church, Sweden 1–3
moths 3, 9, 13–14, 19–20, 23–4, 26, 27, 31, 56, 59–60, 75, 78, 87, 113, 118, 120, 121–2, 143
Munich, Germany 66
Murakami, Haruki: *1Q84* 145
Muslims 146
mycelium 12

Nagel, Thomas: 'What is it like to be a bat?' 12–13
Nakamura, Shuji 179
Narva, Battle of (1700) 137
Nashville, USA 74
Natt ('Night') (Nordic goddess of mythology) 172
nature, sense of well-being and 122
nautical twilight 128
navigation 3, 23–4, 25, 26, 44, 47, 48–9, 71, 72, 73, 78, 95, 128
Newton, Isaac 125
Nicaragua 94
nightjar, European 13, 15, 46–7
night shift 165–7
night vision 12, 13, 17, 43, 44, 46, 52, 78, 138, 149, 176, 180, 184, 193, 201
9/11 77
Nobel Prize 16, 132, 175
  Physics (2014) 179
  Physiology or Medicine (2017) 7
Noche Zero 177
North American Bat Conference 48
northern bat 60, 118, 191
northern lights (*aurora borealis*) 4, 149–50, 159, 184, 204
North Pole 8, 73
North Star 72–3, 127, 133
Nottingham catchflies 12
nyctophobia (fear of the dark) 17
Nyord, Denmark 185, 186, 187

oak tree 12, 82
obesity 18, 165–6
observatories, city 151–2
Odin 150
Ogden, Sweden 78
oil rigs 108–9, 199
optic nerve 41
Öresund Region 129
Orion 73
orsten or 'stink stone' 40
owl 45–7, 51, 60
owlet moths 13, 120

Pacific Ocean 97, 101, 103, 177, 178, 183
palolo worm 103–4
Peebles, James 131–3
perch 107
Perseids 140
Perseus 140
Persson, Johan (Lill-Jan) 190
pesticides 119, 120, 122
Phanerozoic era 37

pheromones 26, 27
Philippines 63
photography 83
photons 17, 24, 38, 41, 42, 125, 133, 161, 179
photosynthesis 9, 101, 103
phytochromes 83, 85–6
pineal gland 67
pipistrelle bat 191
Planet Earth II 93
plankton 106
plants
  circadian rhythm and 7–9
  greenhouse 85
  long-day growth 86
  photosynthesis 9, 101, 103
  phytochromes 83
  pollination *see* pollination
  seasons and 81–4
  short-day plant 85–6
Pleiades 137
Plough 73
poachers 53
poinsettia 85, 86
polarised light 23–6
polar light/polar night 127, 147–50, 184
pollination 3, 9, 13, 14, 31, 32, 53, 86–7, 120, 122, 200
pollution, light 2, 3, 4, 5–33, 57, 79, 94, 100, 103, 108, 129, 136, 166, 174, 177, 186, 187, 199, 201, 204
  circadian rhythm and 7–10
  experiences in darkness and 11–14
  illuminated planet 15–18
  mass die-off and 29–33
  mating impulse and 23–7
  term 4
  vacuum cleaner effect and 19–22, 75
  See also individual effect of light pollution
predation 3, 9, 37–8, 49, 52, 53, 55–6, 58, 59, 63, 67, 86, 89, 107–8, 111, 112, 113
Princeton University 131
prostate cancer 166
pupil 41, 42

radio waves 126
Ragnarök 150
ragworm 104
Ramadan 146
rats 45, 56, 112–13
red light 57, 91, 126, 147, 161, 184
red poinsettia 85
reproductive cycles 32
retina 38, 41–3, 46, 71, 149, 161, 176
rhodopsin 17, 43, 149, 177
rice 119–20
ridley sea turtle 94
Rocky Mountains, USA 79
rödfyr 38–9
rods (photoreceptor cells) 42–4, 46
Romanes, George John 19–20, 75
Rømer, Ole 125
Roppongi Hills, Tokyo 175–7
Rosbash, Michael 7
Rosendal Palace 189
Roskilde, Treaty (1568) 185
Rousseau, Jean-Jacques 157
rowan tree 82
Rydell, Jens 116, 206

Saint Lawrence's tears 139–41
Saint Lucia's Day 147–8
salmon 107
Salt Lake City 78–9
Sargasso Sea 95, 141
SARS-CoV-2 virus 119
satellite pictures 15–16
Sauer, Eleanor and Franz 72–4
Säveån, River 107
Saving Nemo Conservation Fund 98, 99, 100
Scripps Institution of Oceanography, San Diego 91
sea anemone 98–100
sea-fire 12, 89, 91, 92

seals 107, 191
seasons 21, 67, 82, 159–63
sea turtle 93, 94, 97
sea urchin 108
Secret Life of the Cat, The (BBC documentary) 52
security 107, 173, 180, 186–7, 193, 200
sex cells 102–4
sextant 128
sexual maturity 67, 68, 98
ships 91, 108, 109
shooting stars 139–41
shops 67, 93, 148, 156
short-day plant 85–6
Singapore 17
singing, wrong light and 55–8
sixth mass extinction 31
Skansen, Sweden 190–1
Skjálfandafljót, Iceland 19–20
skyglow 57, 77, 113
sleep 7, 8, 14, 17, 18, 32, 51, 55, 82, 143–4, 149, 155, 158, 161, 162, 163, 165–7, 196, 203
Slottsskogen Observatory, Gothenburg 151–2
smog 157
snow 159–60
Sol ('Sun') 172
sonar 48, 108
songbirds 11, 65–7, 74
South Pacific Current 97
space dust 146
space telescopes 132
Spallanzani, Lazzaro 47
sparrow 68, 111
sperm whale 90–1
spider worm 61
spiders 12, 25, 32–3, 56, 61
spring 45, 61, 65–9, 81, 82, 104, 115–16, 127, 149, 160, 162, 174, 187
spring equinox 127
Stagnelius, Johan 172
starfish 89, 99, 105
STF Aurora Sky Station 184
Stjerneborg 129
Stockholm Exhibition (1897) 189
streetlights 3–4, 10, 15, 17, 21, 51, 56, 57, 63, 82, 83, 87, 91, 93, 113, 159, 160, 162, 180, 181, 186, 199, 201, 204
stress 165, 195, 197
Strindberg, August 157–8, 190
sun
  bird navigation and 71
  moon's reflection of light and 143, 145, 146
  polar night and 148–9
  sunstone 24
  twilight and 126–9, 204
  vitamin D and 160–1
  zodiacal light and 146
suprachiasmatic nucleus 161
Svartklubben, Stockholm 196–7
Swedish Civil Aviation Administration 127
Swedish Lapland 184
Swedish Museum of Natural History 22
Swedish Red List 117, 118–19
Swedish Work Environment Authority 156
Swift, Lewis 140–1
Swift-Tuttle comet 139–41

tammar wallaby 68–9
Tanizaki, Junichiro: *In Praise of Shadows* 175–6, 193
tapetum lucidum 43, 46
Tasmania 61–2
Teide 183–4
Tempel-Tuttle comet 141
Tenerife 183–4
Tessin the Younger, Nicodemus 137
Thailand 119–20
Tidaholm, Sweden 115, 155–6
tidal zones 104
tiger 113

Tolken, Lake, Västergöötland 139–41
tourism 61, 62, 74, 94, 99, 100, 121, 189
  darkness 183–7
Tracy Aviary 78–9
trees, seasons and 81–2
Triangulum Galaxy (Messier object 33) (M33) 136
Triassic Period 93
Tribute in Light 77
Tromsø, Norway 184
Turkey 94
Tuttle, Horace Parnell 140–1
twilight 2, 11, 13, 15, 26, 59, 60, 62, 74, 86, 118, 145, 150, 153, 163, 180, 204
  amateur astronomical twilight 128
  animals and 51–3
  astronomical twilight 128, 143
  civil twilight 127–8, 163
  nautical twilight 128
  three phases of 125–9
twilight zone, sea 105–9
Tycho Brahe Museum 128–9

Ulriksdal-Haga-Djurgärden-Brunnsvike, Sweden 189
ultraviolet light 12, 42, 57, 87, 126
universe, origin of 132–3
University of Gothenburg 56
unnecessary light 79
US Navy 91
Uyuni 183

vacuum cleaner effect 21–2, 75
Valkyries 150
van der Rohe, Ludwig Mies 180
Västgätaslötten, Sweden 116–17
Vega 127
Venus 137–8
Vienna, Austria 186
Vikings 24, 150
vitamin D 160–1
vitreum 41
Völker, Michael 121
Vordingborg, Sweden 185

Waitomo, New Zealand 61
Wasatch Range, USA 79
water surfaces 24, 26
wavelengths, light 33, 42, 48, 57, 59, 69, 82–3, 126, 167
wave, light as a 125, 126
wealth, light as symbol of 200
West Nile fever 68
weta 111–13
white campion 13
wind farms 109
windscreen phenomenon 29–30
winegrowers 121–2
winter 27, 65, 67, 68, 71, 78, 81, 82, 106, 127, 143, 148, 150, 155, 159, 160, 162, 184, 187, 191, 196, 204
winter solstice 150
wolf's tail 146
World Wildlife Fund 201

X-rays 126

yoga 144
Young, Michael W. 7–8

Zealand, Denmark 184–5
Zeiss telescope 151
zodiacal light 136, 138, 146, 157